ELEMENTS OF ANGLING

ELEMENTS OF ANGLING

John S. McChesney

Beech Publishing House
15 The Maltings
Turk Street
Alton
Hants GU34 1DL

© **John S. McChesney 1992**

This book may not be reproduced or stored in any way without the express permission of the publishers in writing

ISBN 1-85736-041-9

First published 1992

DURHAM COUNTY LIBRARY
ACC. No. 5034045.
Class No. 799.12

Beech Publishing House
15 The Maltings
Turk St
Alton
Hants GU34 1DL

ACKNOWLEDGEMENTS

Thanks are due to my daughter June E. McChesney for all the photographs except the cover which is reproduced by kind permission of <u>Ayr Advertiser and Carrick Herald</u>

DEDICATION

This book is dedicated to a loving and considerate wife, Jett, who could be classed as an "Angling Widow" for over 40 years

CONTENTS

		Page
1.	Selection of Suitable Equipment	4
2.	Angling for Brown Trout	9
3.	Type of Bait Tackle	17
4.	An Introduction to the Spinning Rod	60
5.	Dry Fly Fishing	76
6.	Pike and Perch	91
7.	Materials for Making Rods	98
8.	Life Cycle of the Salmon	114
9.	Anatomy	117
	INDEX	128

Prize Winners at the local Angling Club (Junior Section)

DOON TROUT

Elements of Angling

INTRODUCTION

During my many years of angling throughout the length and breadth of the country, one of my most interesting observations has been the varying attitudes of beginners as they set out to participate in what is considered by many as the most popular sport in the world. Some are of the belief, that should they acquire very expensive equipment: (rods, reels, tackle, etc.) success is bound to follow. That is not the case, not always. Some will fish during spates only. Even to the extent of fishing over the grass where a river has risen over its banks. Others I have found fishing in streams too small to hold fish. Still others who will splash about causing a commotion and disturbing the water for others following on. Very few are familiar with the etiquette of riverside behaviour when other anglers are about. Some of these misdemeanours have been the source of deep embarrassment to experienced anglers and also to the beginners themselves.

It was with these attitudes in mind, that I felt the need for a simple book on the primary considerations of the sport, which would be beneficial to the young beginner and also for those taking up the sport later in life.

It has been assumed that the new angler will be entering that part of the sport dealing with trout, seatrout and salmon. However for those who might do as I have done, that is break the ice in winter-time so that they can fish for pike and perch there are a few chapters on that side of the sport included.

In addition to simple fly-tying and making simple lures, there are some hints on temporary rod repairs and the care of rods, reels and other equipment.

Should the reader actually be a beginner he will benefit very greatly by going over these pages. The outcome should be a surer confidence while at the water among more seasoned anglers. It should be borne in mind however, that no amount of reading can compensate for the practical experience from the application of know-how over a period of time. From observing keen anglers in action, lessons can be learned also. Treat the opinions of others with respect by giving experienced anglers "a good ear" and be prepared to discuss any theories they might put forward. In this way you will learn more and more quickly than going it alone.

To all who enter here, to take part in the sport for its recreational value rather than for the fame or personal gain it might bring, I would extend my sincerest wishes for success, irrespective of the amount of fish in the creel. Isaac Walton the early writer on the sport, said, "Go forth into the morning light and enjoy many hours at the sport of the angle; the most consuming sport I know".

John S. McChesney
Dalrymple, Ayrshire

Elements of Angling

Great Expectations
A promising glimpse into an 'Angler's Paradise' – Loch Doon

A beginner with ample space to practise casting

PART I

FUNDAMENTAL CONSIDERATIONS ON EQUIPMENT AND TACKLE AND SIMPLE WAYS WITH BAIT AND FLY

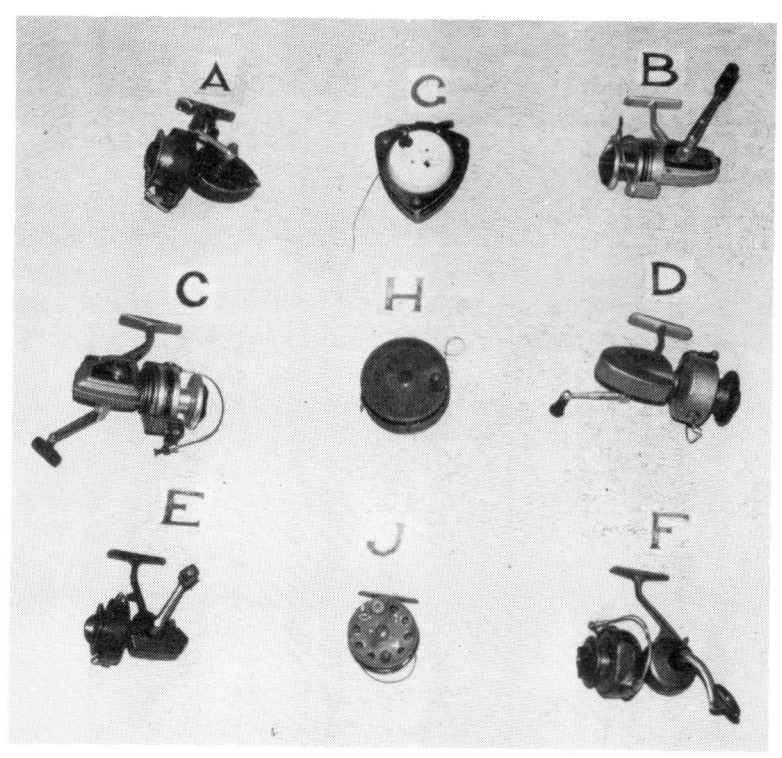

Figure 1.1 Various Reels

Spinning Reels
A   Intrepid Supreme (A T Adjustable Tension)
B   RYOB1 (SX3 ND) A T Capacity Chart on Spool
C   Shakespeare 2711 A T with cap. chart
D   Sup-matic (French) No chart
E   Light weight Shakespeare AT no chart
F   Pinvin 2537 Light weight AT no chart

Reels for Fly Rods
G   ABU Delta 3   3.75 "**
H   Brass Reel 3.5 " Old type, general purpose
J   Aluminium Reel for Trout . 2.50" light weight
** *Salmon Line suitability.*

1
SELECTION OF SUITABLE EQUIPMENT

A Job for the Experienced

The selection of rods and other tackle, particularly for sea trout and salmon, should not be undertaken by a beginner on his own. It should not be assumed that the price will give a complete estimate of the **quality and the suitability** of the rod, reel and line or other tackle about to be purchased. If it is at all possible, attempt to have an experienced angler friend with you when you enter the "Tackle Shop". Of course, it is usual to find that the owner or his assistant are experienced anglers themselves, and therefore willing and often able to give every assistance to the customers. Most of them actually do this, but occasionally an unscrupulous type may not be so honest and try to interest the beginner in old stocks and the less popular types of equipment. Therefore it can be assumed that the young angler with money to spend can be very easily gulled. So enthusiastic can he become in his newly chosen sport that he could accept almost anything.

Having made out the case for having an experienced angler as guide, the bare essentials will be a rod, reel and line, some casts, a few bait hooks and some artificial flies suitable for the three main categories of the sport. A net can be an asset, but a "tailer" or a "gaff" can wait until much later.

The Rod

There are people, who talk of a **general purpose rod**, but I do not wish the beginner to get the idea that one rod will be sufficient for the full range of angling which the tyro might attempt. There are rods for all purposes; however, to begin with, one rod will do well enough. Select a medium lengthed rod between 9 and 10 feet – light and springy, commonly used by the enthusiast when fishing for seatrout, yet able to tackle a fair sized salmon. At the same time, the size of the water to be fished should also be considered. The beginner on a wide water may be better served by a rod around 10 feet 6 inches, both for distance gained for the fly and to reach more places with the bait. In years gone by, split-cane rods were all

Elements of Angling

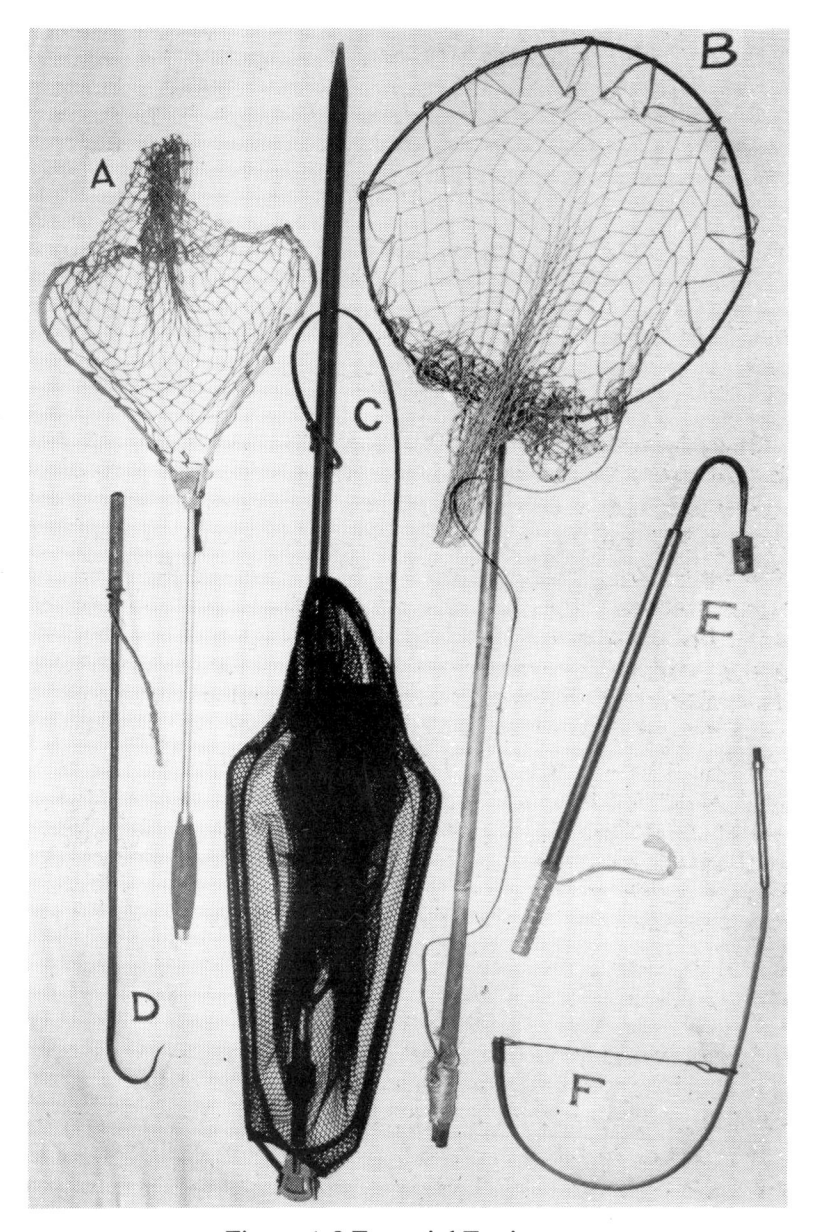

Figure 1.2 Essential Equipment

A Landing Net for Trout (Folding) *B* Landing Net (Net ring screws off for Folding)
C Salmon Net (Folding --used as wading "stick") *D* Simple Gaff (string for wrist)
E Extending Gaff with cork for safety   *F* Tailer (screws on to handle of *B*)

the rage, but during the last decades with the introduction of new materials, flies and lures can be cast as far as was done with the long, heavy greenheart rods of long ago. Glass-fibre and carbon materials introduced to industry in general, have been applied to rod-making also with very striking results. Thus lighter but stronger and shorter rods have become very popular.

The new fly rods of only 12 ft. can cast a fly almost as far and more accurately than a green heart rod of around 15ft or so in length used by our forefathers. Nevertheless some of the older fishermen are reluctant to depart from the hexagonal sectioned split-cane type. The beginner would do well to purchase a rod the size already recommended (9 to 10 ft) and spend a season mastering the techniques of bait and fly casting with it, in varying water and weather conditions before he provides himself with tackle for spinning, more of which in later chapters.

The reel can now be chosen. The size of the reel will be governed by the rod and line chosen to suit the angler and size of the fish expected from the water to be fished. The line could be a No. 2 parallel line – a double tapered line would be better but costs a deal more. The size of the reel should be close to 90mm in diameter and of the ceramic type which is lighter than all metal kinds. To test for suitability – fit the rod together, fix on the reel, which has been filled with line. Thread the line through the rings and take as much through as will reach back to two metres beyond the butt. Hold the rod before you and balance it on one finger at a point 15 cms back from the top-most part of the cork handle grip. If it is heavier at the tip, take off the line and put on some backing line, before putting the line on once more and balancing it again. If it is still heavier at the tip and no more backing line can be put on then a heavier reel is required. If the reverse is the case than a light reel may suit the purpose. Next, purchase a linen or canvas bag to protect your rod during transit. A small bag for the reel also may keep it grit free.

Next, procure a few single bait casts; hooks size 12 or 14 for trout or seatrout and No. 6 or 8 for salmon. They can be got "made up" from the tackle shops, otherwise buy the hooks and nylon of about 6 or 8 B.S. (breaking strain) and make up casts of your own. (See *Bait Fishing*). If they are made up in pairs they are known as **Pennel Casts** ; however if there are three hooks fixed back to back alternately, about 20mm apart , they are **Stewart Tackle**. An experienced friend will dictate the choice of types. Obtain also two casts of flies to comply with the whims of the local anglers. It is usual to have three flies on the cast for trout, two flies on the cast for seatrout and one for salmon. Certain flies are popular in particular waters or areas and with different anglers, but there are numbers which are generally used over most of the country; here are a few – the butcher, teal

Elements of Angling

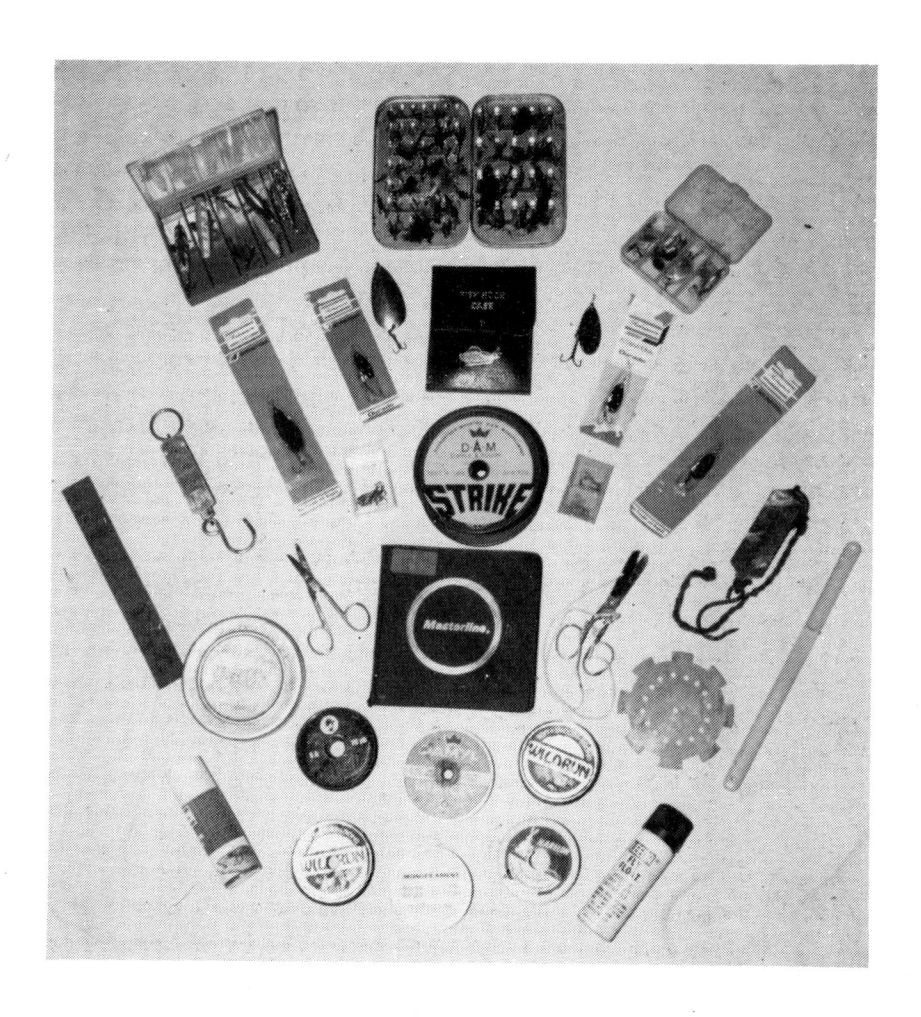

Figure 1.3 Other Essential Equipment

From Top: Boxes of artificial minnows, flies & small spoons, cast case, larger spoons, hooks & swivels, 2 weighing scales, line case, measuring stick, 2 pairs scissors (1 with disgorger), stomach contents extractor, cast box, cast card (plastic), spools of nylon, and 2 sprays (midge repellant & flotant for dry flies).

and green, teal and yellow, teal and some other colours, *Greenwell's Glory, The Coachman*, the dun flies with another section of gnats, nymphs and spiders, for trout and seatrout and for salmon *The Practitioner, Stoat's Tail, Jock Scott*, the *Silver Doctor* and *Brown Turkey*. These are but a few of the types widely used and it is worthwhile consulting the established local anglers before purchasing flies, or other lures likely to be used.

A creel is indeed a very useful item, but can be expensive; therefore in its place obtain a small haversack or knapsack with two compartments – one for catch – "fish" and one for tackle. A pair of scissors should be in the bag but should be attached to the strap with a long stout string. If small scissors can be got with a *disgorger* attached, so much the better. A disgorger can save time for the angler and spare the fish undue pain. If a fish is to be returned to the water in a healthy condition, it will most often suffer less while being unhooked with a carefully used disgorger.

Waders are indispensible to the enthusiastic angler, but one might find, at the outset, that a pair of long stout wellington boots might serve as well. A net is very necessary especially at places where the bank is high or difficult to approach, when a fish has to be landed. A large wide net is preferred but if a smaller one is got, make sure that it is deep enough to take a large fish.

Figure 1.4 Gently flows the Don
Seen from the Bridge at Dalrymple

2

ANGLING FOR BROWN TROUT

When we think of methods which we might employ to lure a beautifully spotted brown trout to our net, we must first of all take note of the many types of food stuffs which a hungry fish will take, and attempt to apply that knowledge to our fishing. There a trout waits head to the current in a stream or at the neck of a pool, its keen eye ever alert to the possibility of a fly afloat on the surface or a nymph moving upwards as it makes its way to participate in a new but limited existence in the ethereal spaces above the water. Similarly it is keenly aware of any unfortunate worm or grub which has dropped from the bank and is being carried down by the flow of water. As soon as the opportunity presents itself, the trout will dart sideways, taste and try, swallow or reject as it thinks fit and then return to its former stance to take up the vigil once more.

Similar circumstances can be located in lochs and reservoirs where there are seemingly no currents, but which are there nevertheless. In heavy rains when the excessive water causes sediments to gather at the inflows of lochs, trout are to be found with their noses to the current as in a stream waiting for a worm or grub which has been dislodged from the bank of the feeder stream to come their way. In quieter waters, a trout may be seen head down and tail up, grovelling in weed or fine gravel for such succulent luxuries as larvae coepods and other small crustacea, that are found there. Trout have been known to take light coloured snails, but this, as a method of fishing, is severely frowned upon in almost all the localities where I have shown any interest in fishing. No well-meaning angler would stoop so low. Some larger trout will be taken by means of artificial flies and some will go for salmon fry or the common minnow. Some may stalk a shoal of these beautiful little fish and having cornered several of them in shallow waters near the bank, will nab one or two as they dart back to the protection of the larger stones.

Having established these facts about the natural food of the trout we can now make our choice from the vast diversity of methods of presenting real or artificial baits or lures to suit the situation. Herewith are some of the

Where to find fish in the lowest water
Flow ↓

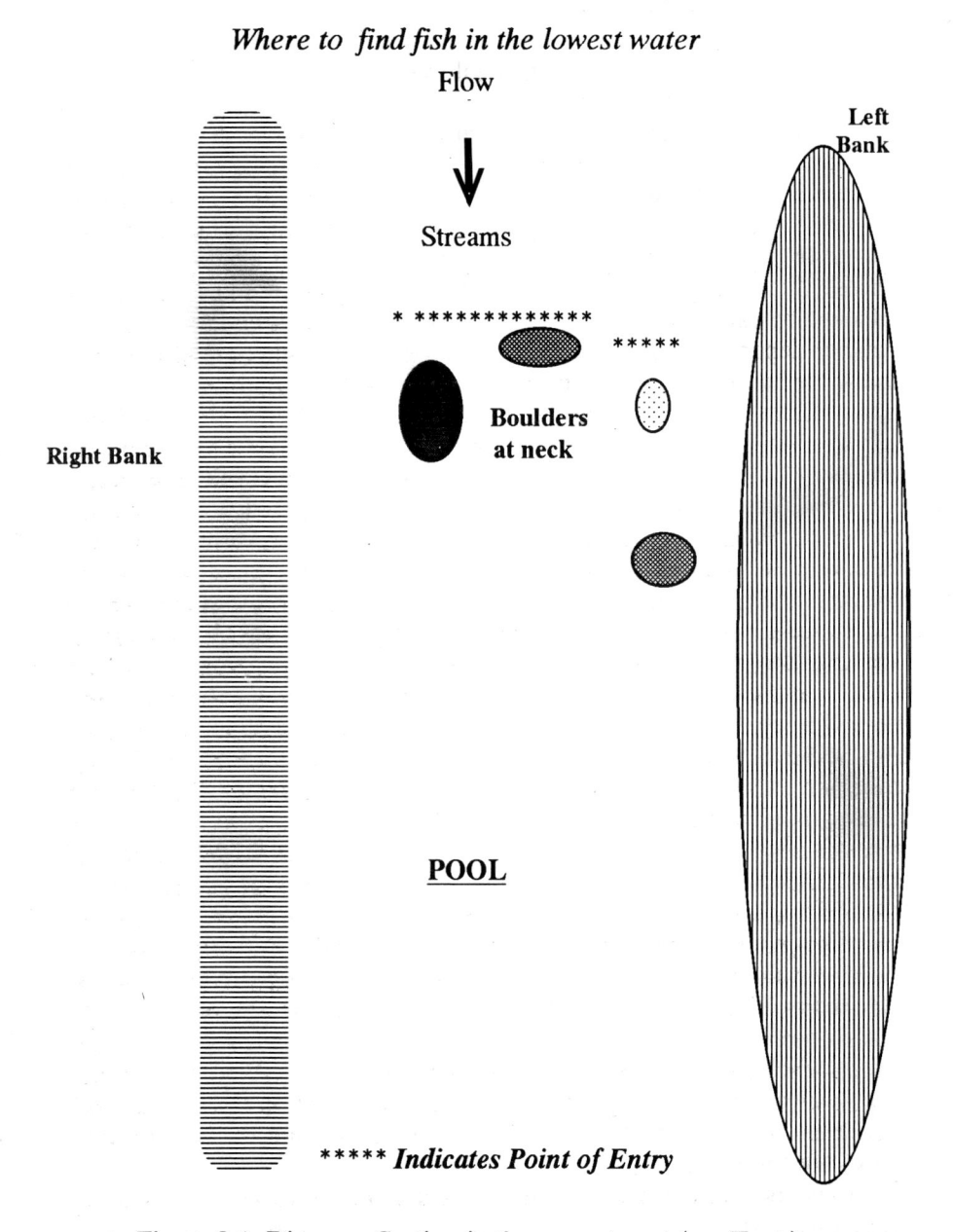

Streams

Right Bank

Boulders at neck

Left Bank

POOL

***** *Indicates Point of Entry*

Figure 2.1 Diagram:Casting in the correct spot (see Text)
Not to scale

Elements of Angling

methods which may be used.

Bait fishing

This refers to the practice of offering some of the fish's natural food on a hook or set of hooks and presenting it in such a way that it seems to have arrived in the loch or stream through the unaided efforts of nature. Therefore great care should be taken to emulate nature as near as possible. Thus when fishing the neck of a pool, in addition to being as inconspicuous as possible, an attempt should be made to have the bait arrive at the point where a fish is suspected to be resting quietly (see figure 2.1). This may be achieved by casting about 2 to 4 metres above the position of the fish, the distance depending on the depth of the water and the strength of the flow. Allow the bait to go loosely down, but also try to keep in touch.

There are times when the bait may be taken immediately and in a very business-like manner, or as my one-time mentor would say "he took it like a man". When the bait is taken in this way, the trout usually is stirred to immediate action, which gives the fisher that sudden thrill of exhilaration only reserved for the ardent angler. A "take" like this usually happens when the bait is only seconds in the water. This can be expected very early in the season or at the first signs of a spate. When the summer sun has caused the trout to seek the more aerated waters in the streamy places, up-stream worming can be tried. Cast in directly above your position, if you are wading, and allow the bait to drift down. Then, by the over-hand retrieve method, keep in touch with it until it is almost directly below you, bringing it slowly towards the near bank where, if at all possible, it should be allowed to remain for a few seconds before the next cast is attempted. This should be done as a fish may have followed it round, suspiciously eyeing it, and yet may still not offer to take it until it has come to rest for about 10 seconds. If nothing happens within that time, take one step upstream and cast again. When the upper limit of the part of the river to be fished is reached, casting can be attempted to reach further out than previously. Still try to keep in touch with the bait, yet allowing it to come down with the current as if it was an item of flotsam. Ultimately the bait will come to a position directly below, where it should remain for the crucial few seconds as before. Walk up the bank to within a metre of the starting point and, casting still further out, cover as much area as possible. If this is correctly carried out, and conditions are good and if there are fish about, it should not be long until results are forth-coming.

The bait in a spate: I believe that the best time to fish the bait is when a spate just begins to show. That is when a little extra debris is seen floating down or when there is the slightest discolouration in the water. The first two hours of a promising spate should not be missed because after that time trout and seatrout seem to have less appetite. However, changing to a large white grub (found at the base of the large wild dock plant "docken" in Scotland) may tempt the reluctant fish to take even though they are full up. It is worthwhile opening one at this stage. The examination of their stomachs may disclose some surprises as to the items a fish can feed on. Do this repeatedly during the early years at the fishing, taking notes of the multifarious food stuffs which go to make up the fish's diet.

When your favourite stretch of water will be about to receive the benefit from heavy rains which have fallen further up country, establish yourself at the entrance to a suitable pool and stay there unless there are other anglers present, when the etiquette of the moment compels you to move on to seek another promising pool neck.

Figure 2.2 A Sight for Anglers' Eyes
The same stretch in flood seen from the church – seen in photograph in Figure 1.3
The reason for attempting to stay at the same place for some time will

Elements of Angling

become obvious. Nearly all the fish which have been in the pool below will sense the possibility of more food stuffs coming down with the higher flow or migratory fish may once again have the urge to move further upstream and will gather at the neck of the pool waiting for the water to rise sufficiently for the different sizes of fish to move on.

Take up a position on the bank so that you can reach the exact entrances to the pool. Study the currents carefully so that you will fish the most likely places where fish might lie. (See the illustration for the positions of fish in a spate.)

Avoid wading, if at all possible, for the main reason that you may become so engrossed in your fishing that you do not notice that the rising water has picked up some large object which could pick you up in turn for propulsion into the deeper water below. The first signs of a sudden rise in water may not be discerned by the change in the colour of the water but a sure sign is the increase in the size of the debris floatants coming down suddenly. As the water rises cast closer to the near bank and search for protected eddies at the bank itself or where there is a reverse swirling close in.

As the spate gradually falls, casting should be done in the reverse order – that is close to the bank and changing by stages until the fish will be situated in their original positions before the spate started. On rivers of any size subject to very high spate these conditions will be evident, but should the river overflow its banks and your lure is actually fishing on the bank, angling proper becomes impossible, so pack up and go home. Wait for the water to recede and make preparations to spin with minnow mepp or spoon and wait a little longer until the conditions will be more suitable to fish with the fly.

From the fore-going pages it should be evident that the spate-bait fisher should follow his quarry during the rising water by casting nearer and nearer to his own bank so that at its height he will be casting the heavily weighted bait very close to the bank in the quieter eddies. He should place the bait slightly upstream and allow it to move slowly down at the neck of a pool and then cover the pool edge by moving down a step or two for each cast.

Success should come early in a spate by the fish mostly hooking themselves, but when it is suspected that the fish are only sort of tasting the bait and letting it pass on because of their diminishing appetite so that only a slight touch is felt, take two or three steps quickly down the stream and with the rod tip almost touching the water strike firmly against the current; it should be obvious why. Even in sheltered corners fish are usually facing the current. However, be careful to avoid striking too firmly for fear of

Elements of Angling

Where to find fish in the **highest** water

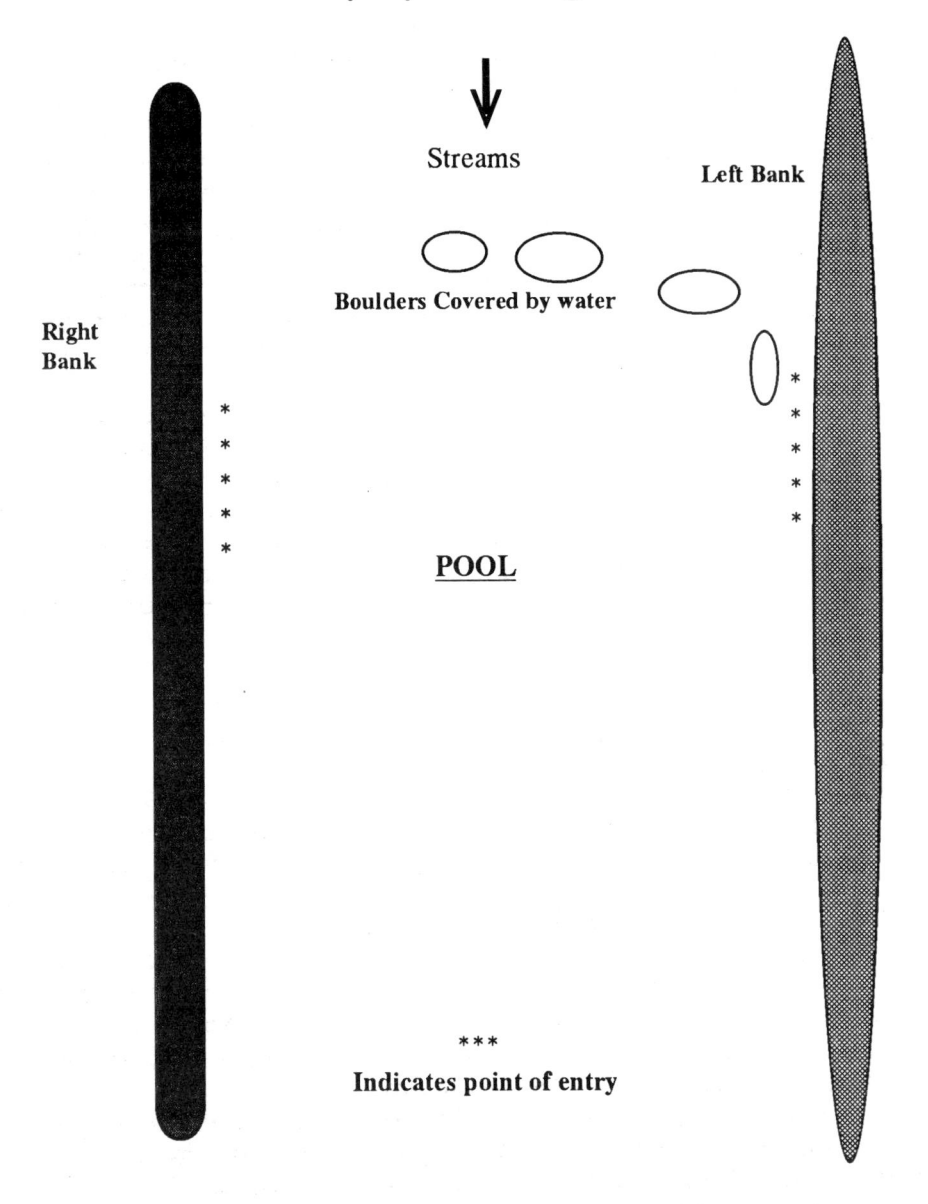

↓

Streams

Left Bank

Boulders Covered by water

Right Bank

POOL

***
Indicates point of entry

Figure 2.3 Diagram: Casting in the correct spot (see Text)
Not to scale

Elements of Angling

emulating the writer when he smashed a small home-made rod on a big fish by being over-anxious as a learner.

Up-Stream Worming

This method has already been referred to. On a narrow burn or smallish river this can best be done from the bank, but for the wider streams of larger rivers, wading will be necessary to reach some distance to the attractive lies. Perhaps the best time of the season for this type of fishing is at the height of the summer, when the sun has heated the water to such an extent, that the fish are found well up in the streamy water above a pool, seeking the extra oxygen which is to be found there, due to the more excessive turbulence at the shallower places. Commence by entering the water just above a large pool in which you have previously seen fish moving and wade slowly and quietly to a suitable spot and extend the casting almost directly above you at not less than 15% to the current.

Have the line and cast about 2 metres longer than the rod and as you cast, the line should be very slightly taut to keep in touch with the bait at all times. To do this raise the rod tip gradually and retrieve line by the overhand twist method. Keep on the alert as the bait swings round to be directly below you. Should a fish be felt while the bait is above you, strike immediately by lifting the rod up suddenly. If you miss, that may well be your last chance at that particular trout or seatrout for you may see a fast moving wake as the fish dashes to the safety of the deeper water.

If a fish is felt when the bait is below you count to three before striking. If a reasonable sized fish is on, make for the bank as quietly as wading will allow to arrive at a point below the part being fished, thus you will be able to fight the fish without disturbing the lies still to be fished. You might think "Why not fight the fish from the place where it is hooked?" Many a fish has regained its freedom by going round a pair of waders. Most experienced anglers get to the bank to enjoy the battle with bigger fish.

Bait fishing on a loch

Although fishing from the loch shore is not very interesting to me, if you wish to have a go, fish with a float and do your best to judge the depth of the water where the bait will be and adjust the float accordingly. Cast out to a distance which will suit a gentle cast to preserve the bait. It may be said that the side cast or side "sling" is the cast to use.

Lift out the bait slowly. Should the float be seen to bob and then go down, strike immediately by suddenly giving a quick push forward away from you. It is difficult to determine the direction in which the fish is facing in still water, but with the aid of the float above, a strong push strike imparted to the hook is usually more successful than the normal strike from the reel.

One method of fishing in still water is to cast out as far as possible – no float – and allow the bait to lie, in the hope that a good passing fish may be tempted. This method does not appeal to the confirmed angler. Some will actually go to extremes of resting the rod on a reed stick stuck into the bank. This is illegal, as it constitutes "set-lining". Nevertheless many would-be fishers practice it. To me it is a waste of good fishing time. I would rather be moving about over a wider area to search for a taking fish.

From a Boat

Success has been gained by fishing bait from a boat, but this is usually frowned upon by the keener type of angler. The bait is cast gently out, is allowed to sink to a selected depth and even in very calm water should be retrieved very slowly. Occasionally fish are taken by slowly trawling the bait behind the boat. In this kind of trawling the bait must be a considerable distance from the boat and moved exceedingly slowly. If two lines are being used with the bait or with any form of lure, the two rods should be placed as far apart as possible and pointing away from one another at the stern. Should a fish be hooked on one, then both rods should be got under control immediately. I can recall an instance when a friend and I were trawling with the fly. As we got out the trawl while returning against the wind for the next drift, my friend was at the oars while I sat at the stern, a rod in each hand, when two good sized trout rose, one to each cast. Before we could bring them to the boat we had to extract our casts from the shore reeds, and the fish were lost.

However, at a later date much the same incident occurred. This time we were more fortunate because it happened near the middle of the same loch and both fine fish were netted. As was already stated not many would dream of trawling with bait. It is however intended to cover many methods of angling, therefore this method is included as an easy method.

Figure 2.4 Mixed bag taken early in the day in a spate
Using bait with a short spinning rod – a salmon of 10 lbs, a sea-trout of 3.75 lbs and a brown trout of 1.25 lbs.

3

TYPES OF BAIT TACKLE

We older anglers are prone to talk about fixing hooks to gut, when we really mean fixing hooks to monofilament nylon. Gut is a thing of the past. Now we find such trade names as "Luron", "Platil" and "Damyl" among others for this very strong material. Using one of the nylon lines of a suitable B.S. (breaking strain) and two out-bend hooks of No. 12 or 14 size we can make a good bait tackle. Take one hook between the finger and thumb or as shown in illustration on page 18 in a fly-tying vice. Lay the nylon along the top as shown at:

(a). and with dark red or light-brown silk thread, wind the silk away from you on the top. Start at the position shown and wind almost to the bend of the hook and finish by putting on three half-hitches to lock thread at:

(b). At this stage take a small brush and put on a coat of cellulose varnish or put on a spot of glue such as Evo-stick and spread it along the full length of the thread. Give it a few minutes to dry. The thread can now be parted or left to fix on the second hook and parted later.

I prefer to tie them separately myself but it matters little which way the work is done. Remove any surplus varnish or other coating lightly using a small piece of newspaper rather than cloth as it is desired to leave a smooth surface thus making it easier to slide on the bait. This tackle, which should now be hooked up to dry completely, is known as "Pennel Tackle". When the hooks are perfectly dry, coil cast round the spread fingers hooks first, then turn the end of the nylon though the loops three times and place in an old envelope or a cast box. If this method of coiling the cast is done regularly in the same way, then, even if it is necessary to change a cast in the dusk or even in the dark, it can be done without looking at it. The automatic ability to change casts is an achievement which calls for great patience before its real potential can be realised.

To prepare tackle of other types such as "Stewart Tackle", which has three hooks and the single bait tackle, the method of making up is very similar to the above. See illustration , Figure 3.3 .

Note: The colour of the silk thread may not seem very important, but by taking note of this small point we show that we are conscious of the fact that nothing should be omitted which might contribute to success. When the thread has been coated with varnish the colour

Elements of Angling

of the thread becomes darker. Therefore it is recommended to use light colours of thread at the outset, but when fishing with large grub, a white or yellow thread is preferred.

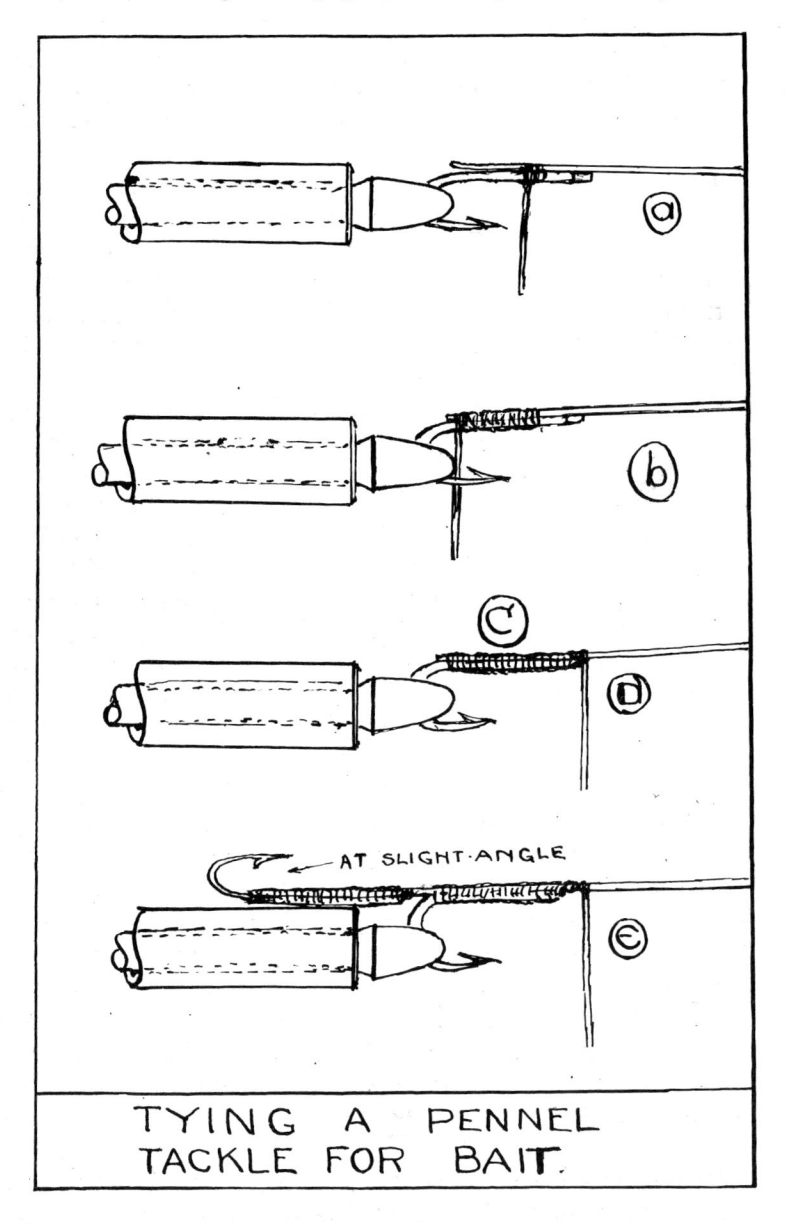

Figure 3.1 Tying a Pennel Tackle for Bait

Elements of Angling

A Few Knots

Strong non-slip knots are very essential to the keen angler and he will meet with a great variety of knots, which are at the disposal of the riverside sportsman. Knots suggested by well seasoned anglers will all have been proved efficient and reliable for their particular methods of fishing, but for the angler who is being catered for here, the number recommended is only five. These are illustrated on pages 20 and 27.

To practice these take a piece of thick string and, with the illustrations before you, (a) and (b) show how to form the loop at the end of the cast to which the line is fixed. Fold in (b) as it is held at (a) to make a very wide loop. Turn it in at (c) at least twice and out at (d) and pull it tightly as at (e) and (d) to take up the position at (g) completing the knot for the end of a cast.

Next knot to attach the other end of the cast to an eyed hook. Thread the nylon through the eye of the hook. Twist nylon four times round itself and finish by passing that end through the space between the hook and the nylon. Hold the end of the nylon under the thumb and pull the nylon tightly. (the nylon is shaded for clarity). You may wish to use an alternative knot to attach the line to the cast. One is shown near the bottom of the page. Observe that the line is shaded while the nylon is unshaded throughout. Enter the free end (r) from the front through the nylon loop taking ample length through- say about 15 cms. Take it down and through the loop. Enter it back through the loop from the same side at (o) to (q) and pull tightly. The end at (r) is cut off, but a portion is left to aid in taking the cast off. These knots, according to research carried out by I.C.I., are estimated to be 85% of the full strength of the nylon. The strength of nylon used for trout need not be more than 6lbs. B.S. and although I have met some anglers who have used nyulon as strong at 36lbs. B.S. for salmon, I have always found that nylon of 10lbs. B.S. has served me well.

Herewith is a tip from experience which serves to save the line while changing casts. With tying and untying line and cast, the line becomes frayed and the frayed portion may require to be removed. This can be minimised by taking a length of slightly stronger nylon (about half a metre) attaching it to the line and then fixing each cast to it. The stronger nylon may gradually become shorter with repeated changing casts, but it can be renewed thus saving the line.

Note: When the end of the season has past, it is advisable to put the line on a line-drier or on a wool-winding frame. Home-made line-driers are illustrated on page 112.

Elements of Angling
Fixing on the bait
Some anglers seem to pay little attention to the method of fixing the bait to the hook, but this is more important than many would have us believe. It must be remembered that our chief purpose is to deceive the very wary fish and if the bait is presented in an unnatural way, the chances of attracting fish will be considerably minimised. On the Plate (Figure 3.3) there are several ways of applying the bait to the hook or hooks. In the case of a single hook this is easily done as at (d) by entering the hook at the end of the bait and "threading" it up the inside until the whole hook is covered.

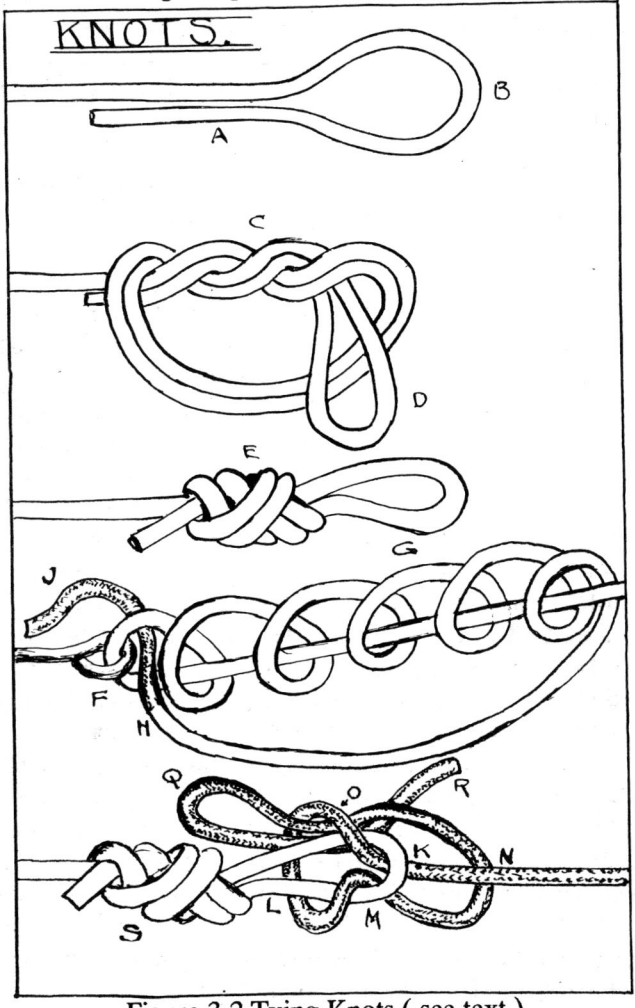

Figure 3.2 Tying Knots (see text)

Elements of Angling

Push on a little more of the bait and cause the point to come out the side of the bait so that the barb of the hook comes to the outside. This will help to prevent the bait from slipping down. It will also expose part of the hook but at the same time increases the chance of hooking a taker. It has proved difficult to impress on some seasoned anglers that this is the best way to work with bait. Their argument is that an exposed hook is easily seen by the fish and that it snags more readily on the bottom, causing the loss of more tackle. Although the second part of this argument can be true, any advantage is outweighed by the number of fish that are lost by the hook slipping from the mouth of a taking fish. This is because the point of the hook is guarded by a cushion of bait flesh between the hook point and the mouth of the fish, and it takes a much more forceful strike to drive the hook home.

At (e) is shown a home made tackle which can be well baited to hide the hooks. At (f) is the ordinary pennel tackle baited in the best way I know. Careless baiting may not affect spate fishing very much, but for up-stream worming every little counts and may be just the difference between failure and success. Notice at (g), that all the hooks are covered except for the points which are exposed. However, if you think the points are too visible, rather than change the method of baiting, make up some casts using a set of smaller hooks. At (a) is the extended Pennel Tackle, which has much to recommend it for all kinds of bait fishing. The hooks are fixed wider apart and this tends to hold the bait in a more natural position. Thus the shank of the hook lies closer to the bait in each case. On the other hand, (b) is a poor method as it is not usual for a bait to float down in the water in this position – this is a poor presentation. The salmon fisher who prefers to "ledger" for taking-fish on the bottom can resort to the method shown at (c), where one worm is threaded on to the hook and up the shank, a second one is threaded up to the bend and the third only passes through to show the barb. Although this is to be recommended, my own personal choice is the extended Pennel Tackle with smallish hooks for nearly all purposes when fishing bait.

Those highly dexterous fishermen, with their nimble fingers, might wish to try using the grub as bait. The grub referred to, is found at the root of the dock plant (docken in Scotland). It can be up to 4cms. long but is very fragile. Use small No. 16 hooks and fix back to back as shown at (e), sketch (Figure 3.3). Fix the grub at the back of the head.

This is the best way to keep the bait from bursting. Of course it will burst whenever a fish touches it, but it is up to the angler to see that a fish does not require to touch it a second time. If you hook a fish every time it is touched then you will be doing very well indeed.

Be prepared to replace bait tackle, for even with the greatest care,

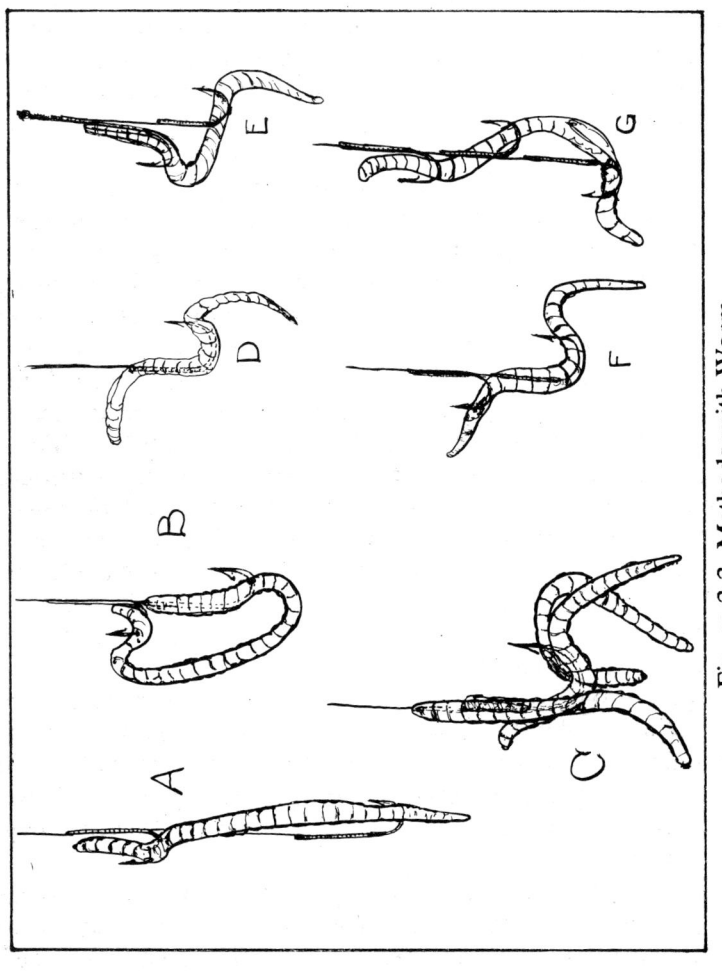

Figure 3.3 Methods with Worm

Elements of Angling

tackle will be lost. To save time, casts made up to your requirements can be carried in a cast box or in old used envelopes. There are also the hungry eels, which are a nuisance from the middle of the season onward and they can very easily spoil your tackle. Here is a hint which might be useful, if an eel should take the bait: immediately an eel is known to be on, attempt to get it to the surface as soon as possible and while it is there, keep jerking the line and cast continually to prevent it from forming itself into knots. If you continue long enough the eel will become exhausted and it will be more easily unhooked.

Preparing the bait

Worms and grubs can be purchased at fishing tackle shops, but anglers resident in the country can easily prepare their own. When the weather has been damp, huge dew worms can be easily collected at night by going out to the garden, especially the lawns with a torch and moving stealthily. Long worms seem to feed half way out on the surface. They should be gripped quickly and held until they give up their grip. If they are gripped too slowly and the greater part of the worm is in the ground, it may part in two. Should this tend to happen let go and seek another. Most of the worms captured in this way are soft and are not suitable for immediate use. They should be hardened off and this is done by adding a little moss to the container and leaving them for at least 12 hours before they are required. If moss is not available some grass cuttings will suffice. The container must have perforations on the lid to allow the free entry of air, otherwise the worms will die for the want of oxygen and will soon rot. The smell should indicate that this has happened.

Large grubs can be obtained as suggested on page 10 and they too require fresh air to keep them happy. They can be kept in bran, oat meal or sawdust to keep them dry and so that they can be more easily handled. To obtain the smaller grubs for night fly fishing, take a piece of old meat or offal and place it in a large deep tin; open at the top to allow the large blue fly access to lay its eggs.

The container should be deep enough to keep out cats or dogs or other animals. Allow this to remain for a few days so that the small resultants grow to fully a centimetre long. These can be gathered and placed in a small suitable tin with bran or sawdust as above. They are excellent for fishing with at dusk and in darkness. Two or three on the fly hook are attractive to both trout and seatrout, but they too must be handled with extreme care to prevent them from being burst. They should be used within a few days, however, as they soon change into cocoons – the next stage in the metamorphosis of the insect.

Casting with the bait

Casting with the bait to cover a wide extent of water calls for a higher degree of skill than might be assumed. One important factor is keeping the bait intact and in good condition while casting to the furthermost places. There are three ways in which this can be achieved:

    (a) The side swing
    (b) The over head cast
    (c) The shoot through method (*See* 'Casting with the fly')

(a) The side swing is by far the best method to preserve the condition of the bait. With the bait fixed, run off line until the total length of line and cast reaches beyond the butt of the rod by about a metre. Hold the rod preferably in the down stream hand about chest high. Take the cast in the other hand around 6" above the bait and with the line pressed against the butt with fore finger, swing the rod from pointing down stream until it points upstream at about 45° to the current and at a low angle. Release the finger immediately and the bait should finish close to the desired point of entry. It is hoped that when a few more casts have been completed a reasonable standard of accuracy will be attained.

(b) The over head cast:

This starts in the same way as the side swing except that the rod is held almost vertically. The bait is held as before but the bait goes across the body and is actually beneath the rod butt. Release the bait as the rod is pushed forward gently at first, gradually increasing the force until the bait reaches the point of entry. Then lift the rod and keep in touch. Be prepared to join a sporting fight with a good fish. However, **if the bait should become snagged,** do not be too impatient about attempting to free it. The tendency of an angler in a hurry is to take a grip on the line and yank it free. Before resorting to the ultimate breaking of the line or cast, a few tips are worth passing on:

    (i)**By putting on a medium strain and suddenly releasing it, I have occasionally been able to save tackle. Sometimes all that is required is to walk well up the bank allowing the line to run out and put a similar strain at a more acute angle.**
    (ii) **Another method which I would try next, is to pull some long grasses or reeds to form a wreath round the line. Then twist them into**

Elements of Angling

a circle and put them on the line beyond the rod-tip. Allow it to go down the line and to float away with it slackened. Take control of the line and at different stages renew the strain and if necessary allow the wreath to reach the snag and a final pull might get the desired result. If not, then the forced break will be the order of the day.

(iii) If strong nylon has been used take the line at the reel, twist it round the arm over the clothing to prevent the line from cutting into the skin, and pull until one of two things happen :
(a) the tackle is freed due to being released *or*
(b) a hook breaks or straightens out when the lure could come flying at some speed and because it could strike the angler on the face or other part of the person it might have been better to turn one's back to the water and cut down the chance of injury.

River-bank Etiquette

Three anglers approach the same point on a river and they intend to use the three main methods of angling – bait, spinner and fly respectively. Who should be allowed to start fishing first? There is an unwritten understanding that the fly fisher goes first, the spinner second and the bait fisher last. This is for obvious reasons – the fly fisher prefers an undisturbed water, the spinner likes to keep moving on and the bait fisher usually prefers to stay longer at one place. This similar understanding applies at other times also. When the fly fisher catches up with the bait fisher, he should be allowed to pass through by the bait fisher who should withdraw his tackle accordingly. In the same way the spinner should allow the fly fisher to pass through also while he in turn should take precedence over the bait fisher.

A very important point not always observed by some anglers (very few in fact). When a companion hooks a fish in the same pool, all other anglers in that pool should withdraw their tackle to allow the fish to be played without being interferred with by other tackle. This also allows them to be ready to assist in landing the fish if requested by the active angler at the end of the line.

Feeding habits

It has long been established, but still considered a peculiarity in nature, that salmon do not take food in our rivers or lochs during the several months they spend waiting to perpetuate their kind. Why then can they be tempted to take the bait in the form of worm, grub or minnow, which has been placed before them? What prompts very large fish to rise from the safety of their secluded lies, to take a very small fly, nymph or spider on or near the surface all lures that are very small in comparison to the size of the

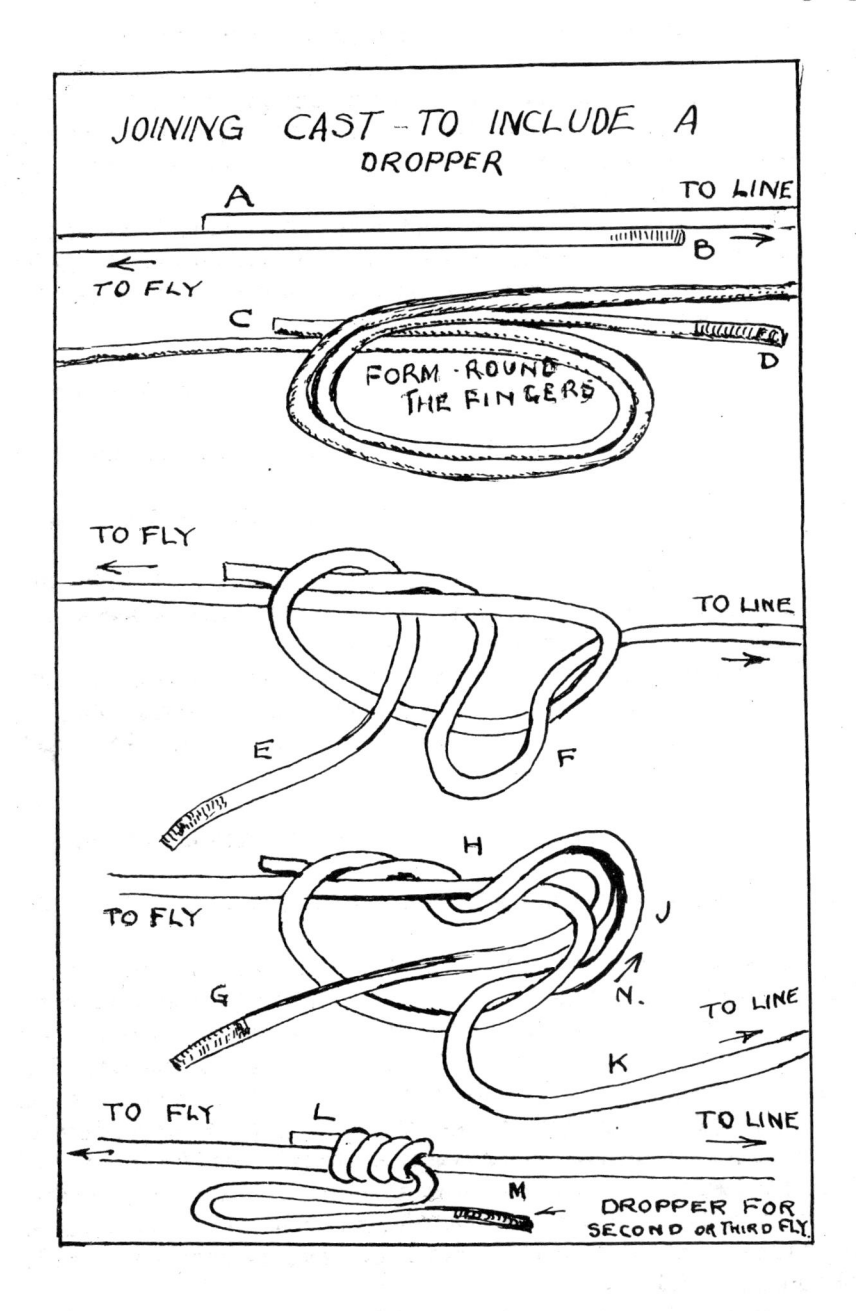

Figure 3.4 Joining Cast to include Dropper

Elements of Angling

fish itself. It does happen and many anglers accept this as a possibility without attempting to understand why. In contrast young parr and smolt feed in fresh water before going off to sea to return in two or three years time when they might weigh 5-6-7 or 8 lbs in weight. What they feed on at sea is not clear. Many assume that they consume large numbers of prawns, therefore some use prawn as bait.

We know more about the seatrout which also returns from the sea. They do feed in the fresh water and their diet is almost identical to that of the native brown trout whose diet I have often noted by examining the stomachs. In one 10" trout I found the following:

(1) Small minnow partly digested. Taken head first and the head almost gone.
(2) Fourteen small shells which I take to be snail shells none more than 4mm.
(3) Three partly digested "horse and carts" commonly called the caddis-fly grub.
(4) Twenty bodies of different sizes of flies – their wings not discernible.
(5) Tiny clusters of gravel, which may have been taken by accident or taken as an aid to digestion as with a fowl.
(6) The remainder (about the same amount again) was so mixed up that I could not identify any more items. There were no worms, which is surprising as there was a slight spate two days before. This could point to very fast digestion.

Attention is now drawn to fishing with the fly and we start with:

Making a fly cast to include a dropper: (See illustrations in Fig. 3.4)

In Figure 3.4 is given a simple but reliable way of joining the lengths of nylon and at the same time leaving a dropper to which the bob or mid fly can be attached. The end indicated as going towards the line is drawn through a double loop (this having been formed over the fingers lettered 'c' and 'd') twice or three times according to thickness of the nylon used shown at (n). When pulling up tightly to close the knot, keep a good pressure on with the finger and thumb. When completed there should be about 4" of nylon remaining for the fly which, when attached, should not be more than 2" away from the knot as, if it is much longer, it is more liable to tangle while casting. Should the hook be fixed, as shown on page 20, it can be easily undone as follows:

Using the nails of the fore-finger and the thumb to grip the knot halfway

Elements of Angling

along its coils, while holding the hook firmly in the other hand and pulling vigorously, the knot should slide apart. This will leave the end of the nylon all curly where it was tied, but if pressed between the same two nails, the curl will be minimised. The nylon will be slightly flattened but will usually still be able to be passed through the eye of the hook. If not however, resort to the use of spare casts (with droppers but without flies) already prepared and carried in a separate box. It is sometimes quicker to take the flies from a tangled cast than to attempt to disentangle a very badly mixed up cast and leave the untangling till home is reached.

Casts can be divided into the following categories:

(1) Parallel casts for trout;
(2) Tapered casts for seatrout;
(3) Parallel casts for salmon;
(4) Tapered cast with graded flies where all three fish types are to be found.

On page 29 see chart of recommended lengths and strengths for the different types of fly casts. The lengths given are only approximate but should serve as a guide until the angler gains sufficient experience to judge for himself which lengths will suit his estimate of the requirements and conditions prevailing. The grades of B.S. recommended are perhaps to the strong side, but it is preferable to use strong casts at the outset and gradually fish finer as time goes by.

For a trout-parallel cast, one of the many types of mono-filament nylons on the market is excellent and tied in the knots suggested should be used. "Parallel" means using nylon of the same B.S. from the line to the top or tip fly. It is often the practice to fish with four flies on a cast but I prefer only three or two. The cast itself can be made up of two or three grades of mono-filament. Casts made in this way have the stronger or strongest nylon next the line. The droppers should be of the stronger material at each joint.

It should be understood that these casts are made up of approximately the same lengths of sections, their full lengths being close to the sizes given in the table on page 29. It is therefore desirable that the lengths of the rod should be taken into account, because a longer cast is much more difficult to cast with, especially with a very short rod.

Because the main advantage of using a tapered cast is that of causing the flies to alight lightly on the surface, its use is uncalled for until the angler has become proficient at casting. It is worth repeating that the droppers for the intermediate flies should be kept to the minimum length to

Elements of Angling

prevent those patience-testing tangles.

TABLE OF LENGTHS FOR MAKING UP CASTS

TYPES

2.50m TROUT	PARALLEL OR TAPERED
2.75m SEA TROUT	PARALLEL OR TAPERED
1.50m SALMON	PARALLEL
1.75M GENERAL	TAPERED

FLIES PER CAST RECOMMENDED

TROUT	THREE	SIMILAR SIZE
SEA TROUT	TWO	SIMILAR SIZE
SALMON	ONE	SIMILAR SIZE
GENERAL	THREE	DIFFERENT SIZES

RECOMMENDED B.S.(BREAKING STRAIN)

TROUT	PARALLEL	4 to 5 B.S.
TROUT	TAPERED	2 – 4 – 6 B.S.
SEA TROUT	PARALLEL	6 – 7 B.S.
SEA TROUT	TAPERED	4 – 6 – 8 B.S.
SALMON		8 to 10 B.S.
GENERAL		2 – 6 – 10 B.S.

FLIES ON THE CAST ARE CALLED:

TAIL	MID	BOB

Figure 3.5 **Table of Lengths** for making up Casts

Elements of Angling

The Tapered Cast

Many anglers use three flies on the cast when fishing for seatrout at night but I prefer a two step tapered cast with only two flies. In this way I have 50% less chance of a second fish taking a free fly when a fair sized fish is already on. There is also less chance of the free hook becoming snagged while playing the fish. Both these circumstances mostly result in failure – the cast being broken by the fish fighting each other. When the fish are of the smaller size the cast might hold and more than one fish may be netted by taking the one which is further away on the cast first. Because it is more difficult to net fish in the darkness, I try to make allowances for such an emergency by fishing with a slightly stronger nylon. I also use stronger casts if fishing in strict-water. Casts for river fishing should be a bit stronger than would be used on a loch.

Where one is fishing a beat for the first time and little is known about the water or the type and size of fish expected, the three sectioned taper cast with three flies of distinctly different sizes (for trout, seatrout and salmon respectively) is recommended. It is usual to find that the three types of fish will rise to their own particular size of fly selected for them, but of course this is not always true. A friend of mine was fishing a beat for the first time and he used a tapered cast with three graded flies. A salmon of around 9-10 lbs took seatrout fly and almost immediately a seatrout of about 5 lbs took the trout fly. The fight did not last long. There was a great common struggle in which he could not take part and in a few seconds he was left with only one section of the cast on which the salmon fly was still attached and in a few seconds more, there was a violent disturbance some ten metres out and then complete silence. My friend assumed that they were attached to one another but being able to put a direct pull, the cast soon gave way. So it is with fishing at any time: the unexpected incident adds to the excitement and the thrill of angling.

Making a pair of Fly-tying pliers

You will not be long at the "Angle" until you will wish to try tying artificial flies for yourself. If you have already been making your own bait tackles, you will find that the tying of flies will come more easily and now you will wish to furnish yourself with a small pair of Fly-tying pliers. They may only cost a few pence to buy, but there is a great satisfaction in making a pair by yourself.

Obtain a length of copper, brass or galvanised fence wire about 10s.w.g. and of about the length suggested in Figure 3.6. Flatten one end as at (A) for about 20mm and, when flattening the other end, make sure that they are exactly in the same plane (in line). Take small ward files and shape

Elements of Angling

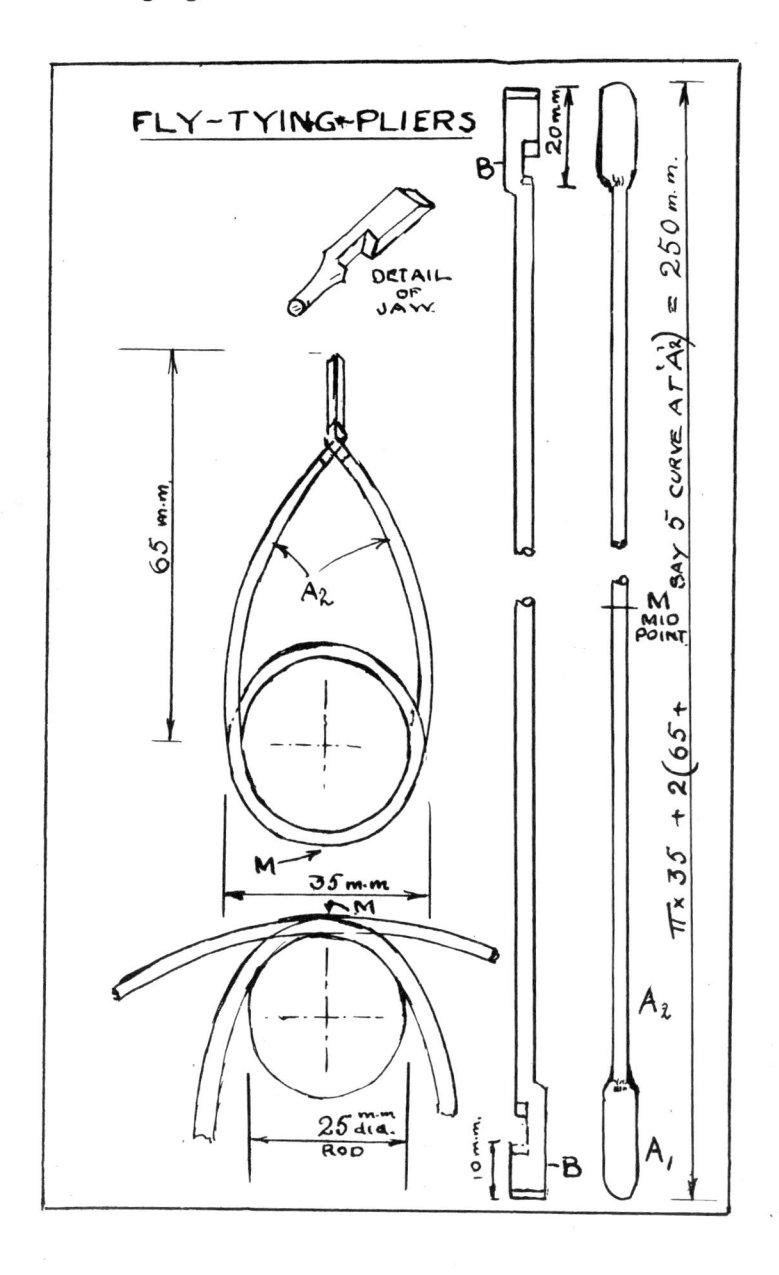

Figure 3.6 Drawing for Fly–Tying Pliers

both ends as indicated at (B). The jaws will be identical in shape to fit into one another. The gap in each should be at least three times the thickness of the flattened wire to give ample movement when they are in use. Next mark the mid-point at (M) on the wire. Procure a former, such as broom handle or other cylindrical object, and mark (M) on that also. Grip the shape in the vice with the marks together and bend the wire round the former taking the ends a good way past one another. Take the jaws past one another on the wrong side meantime. Line them up with two pairs of ordinary pliers. Bend back both ends so that they are almost parallel, with the tips coming together slightly before the rest of the meeting surfaces. Allow these parts to pass on the correct side, after they have been pulled apart to put on a gripping tension. It is with the very tip of the jaws that the holding is done, when they are in use. Now they can be tested. This is done by obtaining a short piece of the silk thread used for fly-tying. Allow the jaws to grip the thread and hold it while the newly made pliers dangle below. Should they fall off, take the jaws apart and give them an extra pull to increase the tension. The thickness of the wire and the length can vary. I have some small pairs which were made from 22 s.w.g. copper wire, which serve me.

Off season activities

To obtain greater enjoyment from angling, the beginner is well advised to indulge in some of the many forms of off-season activities which go along with the sport. To stimulate enthusiasm and to foster the true angling spirit some such activities are included in this book. Instruction is now given on repairing and making up tackle, repairing rods and balancing them. The handling of the multi-various types of artificial flies alone, can captivate the imagination of the beholder and particularly those on the threshold of a life-time at the sport who are setting out on the intricate path of attempting to tie flies, which might lure the big trout or the noble salmon to the net. I well remember my first impressions as I gazed, in wonder, on being introduced to the sight of singularly beautiful glittering tinsel, sparkling hackles and the attractive colours of man-made flies. Even with the advance of time, there still is a bewitching bewilderment which puzzles and delights me as I am permitted to look into some other anglers "box of tricks". I often wonder how any fish can turn up its nose at such alluring creations. How can it possibly resist them? They often do and it is the ambition of many anglers to find out why the fly is not touched at seemingly suitable times. There are literally hundreds of named flies and many more which are unnamed. Some have been "invented" (designed) by individuals, - game-keepers, bailiffs and gillies and are still to be named. Who knows? Perhaps, one day the reader will wish to try a design of his own also;should

Elements of Angling

it prove it to be successful he or she will give it a name.

Some flies are named according to the materials used in their make-up, for example: "Teal and Green", "Woodcock and Yellow", "Grouse and Claret". Some are named after their Inventor, originator, or after some angling personage e.g. "Jock Scott", "Peter Ross", "Tup's Indispensible". Others again are given choice names in other ways such as "The Butcher", "The Highlander", "The Coachman" and on it goes – ad infinitum. Two names, which I have given to successful flies of my own design, are "The Merry Widow" and "The Black Magic" but perhaps more on these later. When one reads in periodicals for advice on the use of flies, some are advised for use on highland lochs, it can be seen that others are recommended for lowland streams. Then again some other authorities might reverse the recommendations so that it all becomes very confusing at times. I myself take a good look with just a little of the Nelson-eye, because usually little is said of the proportions of fishing times put in during the use of a particular fly. This is very important in assessing the value of any fly. There is also the desire to fish certain flies under certain conditions and at certain times during the season. Thus one can find cause for putting the flies into many categories – loch-flies, river flies, ones for night fishing, for early season, mid season or late season, all with further sub-divisions e.g. spiders, gnats, spinners, nymphs and so on. No matter which particular type of fly we use, each and every one is intended to simulate some form of fly, chrysalis, grub and what-have-you and there are many methods of attempting to produce a true likeness.

In different parts of the country the same artificial fly may have a different name. So also with the different parts of the fly itself. All this is quite permissable and understandable but is also regrettable and very confusing to many a tyro. Names like body, thorax, barrel, tube, and similarly quill flies, belly, settae, tail, whisks etc. can become more confusing than useful to the young starter. In our instruction we will not be over ambitious with names and at any rate simplicity is usually the best.

If, after you have gone over this long-winded dissertation on the confusion which reigns in the fly tying world, you still wish to tie flies, then proceed.

The basic principle in making an artificial fly is to attempt to establish contact with the trout by luring it to partake of something, which it thinks is its food, and is mistakenly taken for a succulent morsel enjoyed before. The main idea is to have the fish take a hook well hidden or at least partly obscured by the dressing. To do this an almost unlistable supply of materials are used. I say "unlistable" advisedly, as who among us could possibly know all the materials used in the skilful art of tying flies? We,

Elements of Angling

while in practice and in study, will confine our list of materials to a workable minimum, but at the same time mention will be made of alternative materials at our disposal.

Note :Although most people use a fly-tying vice for nearly all sizes of hooks (see Figure 3.7), and I now do it myself, this is an expensive item, which can be dispensed with meantime. The fingers of the manipulative hand will suffice and will contribute admirably to the tying of the smaller types of fly.

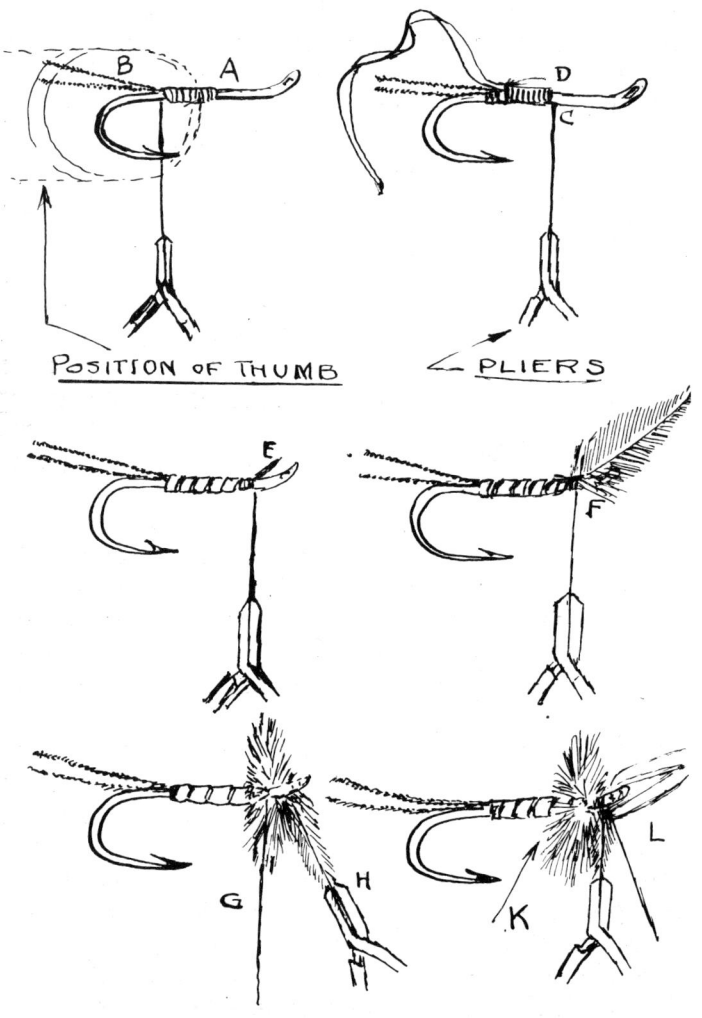

Figure 3.7 Fly-Tying Procedures (Basics)
Fly Tying

Elements of Angling

Fly Tying

A list of tools required as a minimum are: A pair of fly-tying pliers as (figure 3.6), a small pair of finely pointed scissors, a long needle or knitting pin with a sharpened point and a box to hold these items. Gather round you wing feathers, tail feathers and neck hackles of almost any type of birds you can obtain. Any of the following will be useful: hen, cockerel, goose, owl, woodcock, pheasant, partridge, teal-duck, grouse, crow, jackdaw and any others available. As for silks, three of contrasting colours are ample. Choose reels of tying silk, for example one from black or grey, one from green or blue and one from red or orange. A white or yellow could be added but it is not essential. To complete the list we need a reel of narrow gold tinsel and one of silver, a few short pieces of coloured wool, a piece of short fur, rabbit's or hare's lug, and a small piece of beeswax or candle wax.

Where a course is being run and a few are gathered together for the purpose of tuition on this subject, two methods can be employed to gather materials: (1) each individual be delegated to bring a few of the items listed and pool the resources, or (2) the instructor can purchase the whole list of requirements and divide out the cost among those participating. The second method is the surest but the first opens the way to the young ones finding materials for themselves. The choice of size of hook is quite important. A small hook usually makes the work more difficult and a large hook will seldom be used by a beginner at the water's edge. No. 12 or 14 will be found to be most suitable with the normal round bend. I have seen a few start with the sneck bend only because they had difficulty in procuring the former. Some horse-hair and tinsel from Christmas wrapping added, will help to cut down the cost for fly-tying materials. Fly No. 1 is in a way not a fly because it is called a "Black Spider". It is also identified as the "Black and Silver Spinner". Before trying to "dress" it from the instructions in Figure 3.7, set out all the necessary materials given in the specification on the table or desk in front of you. The Specification is: **Black Tail, Silver body, Black hackle** (if from a black cockerel it may have a ruddy tint through the tips of the feather) **black or dark-blue silk thread.** The thread should be from 50 to 60 cms and the hackle from 8 to 10 cms. Grip the thread (silk) in one hand and with the wax in the other pass the thread over the wax in such a way that it cuts into the wax very lightly, repeat this three or four times, change the thread end-to-end and repeat. This is done for two reasons: (1) the silk gets a better grip on the hook and on the dressing materials and (2) the silk helps to waterproof the whole of the materials used. Thus the fly will have a longer life. Place the hook point downward between the finger and the thumb (Figure 3.7) and hold the hook at right angles to your vision. Pressing the end of the silk between the thumb and the finger and wind it

Elements of Angling

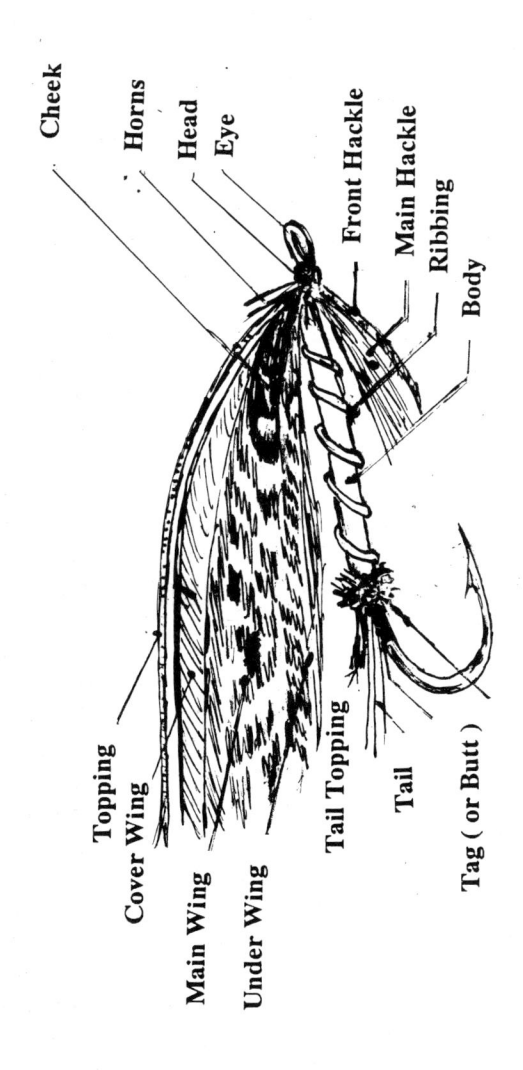

Figure 3.8 Terms Used for an Artificial Fly

Elements of Angling

away from you on the top. Put on several turns and fix by means of the half hitch by pointing out the third finger and putting one turn round it and then passing the silk through the gap between that finger and the hook. Pull it up tightly, but not too tightly to break the silk. Take two fibres of black feather from the tail or wing of fowl, place them beside the hook one on each side (two on each side if desired) and fix them with a few turns of silk adding one or two half hitches.

A piece of silver tinsel is placed on top of the hook pointing towards the bend. Allow the silk to hang below by the use of the fly-tying pliers as shown. Now hold the tinsel on top of the hook and fix it with a turn or two of the fly-tying silk as shown. Now turn the tinsel along the hook and fix it with a turn or two of the silk, and one half-hitch, and then wind the thread all the way along the hook until the eye is only about one mm away, (two half-hitches will secure it there). Fix on the pliers once more and take a firm hold of the tinsel and wind it along the body of the hook until the same place is reached. Fix it there with the silk and then secure with two or three half-hitches. The tinsel can be cut off very closely to the body. The hackle is now to be prepared so put down the hook as it is. Take the selected hackle, which should be of consistent form all the way along. Strip off the fibres from the quill end, so that the good strong fibres remain. Place the quill end on top of the hook and secure with the silk with three to four turns. Allow the silk to dangle again and with the thumb and finger, or a second pair of tiny pliers, twist the hackle away from you on the top. Note how the fibres of the hackle will spread round the body and point outwards as shown. When satisfied that sufficient hackle has been put on, secure the remainder to the body with the silk and finish with three to five half-hitches, carefully cutting the remainder of the hackle. Fine pointed scissors are required here to prevent cutting some of the fibres which should remain. Should the end of the fibres be trapped under the silk, take the needle, knitting pin or a stylo, and pick them out to the surface to obtain a complete circle of fibre equidistant from the body all round. To complete the artificial lure a drop of clear varnish or some form of fixative can be put on by means of a match-end to the last strands of the silk. This will help to preserve the silk and give a kind of shine to form the head. Cut away the silk and now estimate if you have mastered the art of fly-tying. If unsatisfied, scrap it and try another. May your fingers be nimble to produce a thing of beauty! Where anyone has difficulty in following what is taking place, due to failing light or poor eyesight, a sheet of white paper placed beyond the work on the table or bench will be very beneficial.

Having tied several of the wingless types, the beginner should promote himself and attempt an artificial fly with a wing – a "fly-proper".

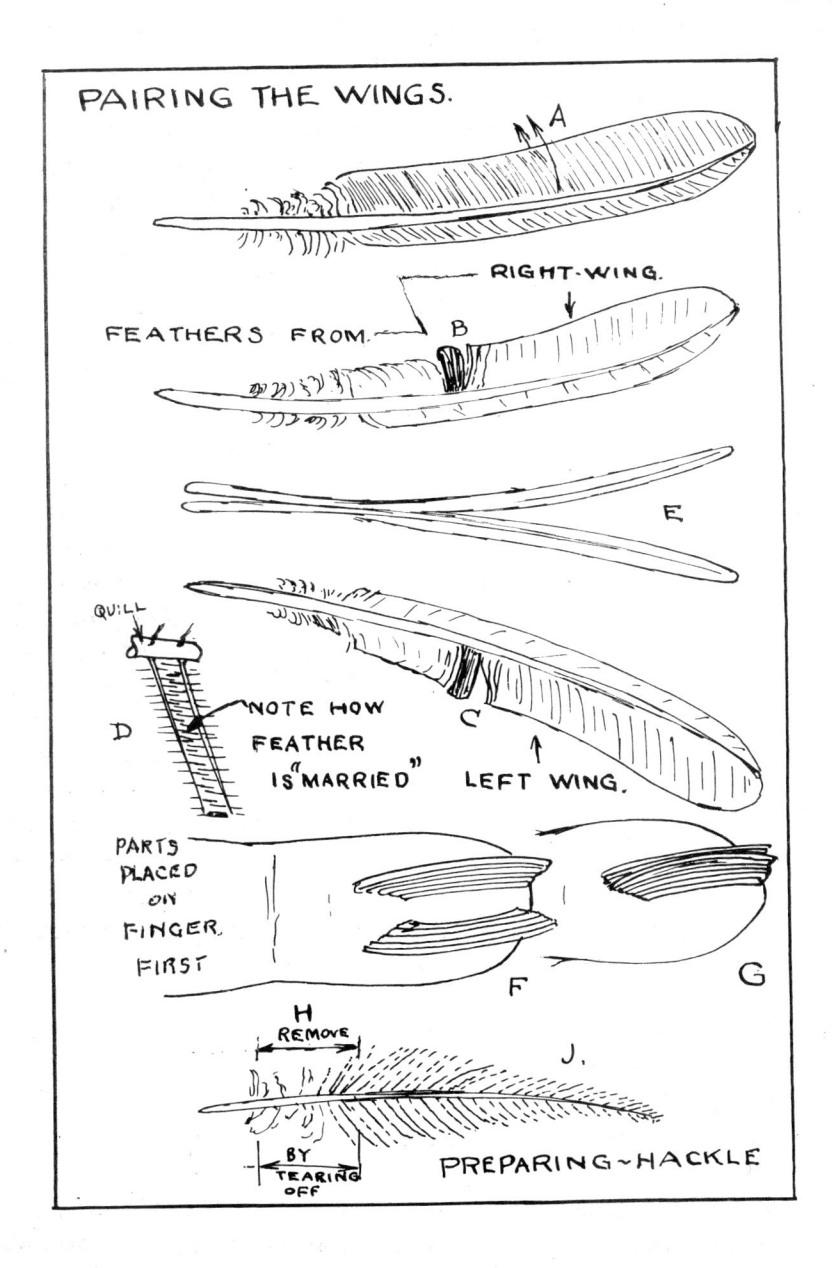

Figure 3.9 Taking Pairs from Feathers

Elements of Angling

deal with pairing and tying the wings of a salmon fly. Although the second is on the salmon fly, the principle is the same for the smaller flies. Once you have the size of hook and the types and colours of feathers chosen, go over the feathers for faults. If any fibres are injured or missing or any parts are displaced, pass the finger and thumb carefully over the feather, one on each side and, with a light equal pressure, attempt to "marry the strands". On occasion, a fibre or two will come away. It is better to discover this fault now, rather than discovering it after all the work has been skilfully completed. Now select a "pair of feathers". (By a "pair of feathers" it is meant two identical feathers, one from each of a pair of wings from the same bird). On the occasions that an identical pair cannot be found, proceed as follows: pair several wings with right and left curves, (i.e. wing feathers from opposite wings of the same bird) and place them face to face or back to back shown at (E) or at (B) with (C). Now cut, with the finely pointed scissors, from 6 to 8 strands from the corresponding position on each feather. These can be set aside until the remainder of the fly is prepared in the same way as the body was made for the "Spider". When you get to that stage you can put on the hackle as was done to complete the type. Looking at illustrations (F) and (G), pair up the wing fibres by placing them on the finger as shown and bring them together to face one another. Place them on top of the fly body or, as some prefer, place one on each side. Hold them firmly and, taking the silk, pass it between the **thumb** and the hook and draw tightly over the top and down the other side between the **finger** and the hook pulling it up tightly – examine (G) and (H) in Figure 3.10. Repeat this several times and if the hackle is already on, put on a few more turns to form a head and finish off the fly as before with a spot of celere varnish. If the hackle is not on, it can be put on now, as was done for the Spider. Herewith is the method of writing up the specification for a fly of this type, the ***Silver Butcher*** :

    Tail = white wing dyed red 4 strands
    Body = silver tinsel, solid
    Wings = black – hen or crow
    Hackle – white cockerel dyed red.

This fly is a great favourite over a wide area of Scotland and comes under the name of the *Bloody Butcher* if the body is changed. (See page 43) When one wishes to tie larger flies, sealing wax can be used in place of the varnish. The wax is held over a candle and a small piece of the softened

Elements of Angling

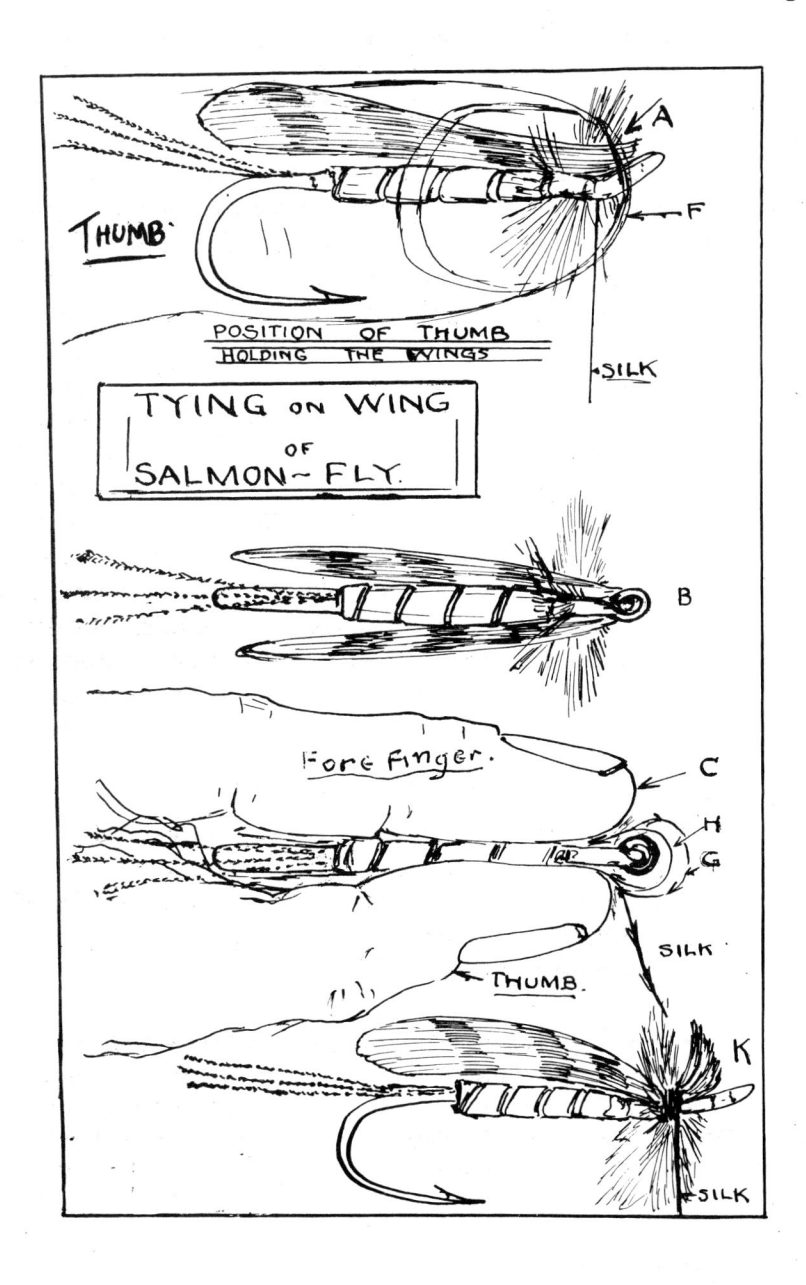

Figure 3.10 Tying on Wing of Salmon Fly.

Elements of Angling

wax removed by means of a match, quickly placed in position at the head of the fly and moulded on by the match. Towards the end of the optional effort to form a head, the fingers can mould a finer form before the wax sets hard. Some of the wax may stick to the metal hook and block the eye – here is another use for the needle or stylo. Should one such blocked eye be missed, then, when discovered at the waterside, another hook can be used to clear it.

As was given earlier, there are literally hundreds of designs of flies on the market, so many that much confusion results. The best method for a beginner is to allow himself to be guided by the older established anglers or obtain a copy of some reliable text on the subject. Comprehensible lists are given in Hardy's *Anglers' Guide* in which one list of over 70 flies is arranged according to the months in which they have proved most successful throughout the length and breadth of Britain. I myself can get by with a few – just over two dozen flies, but of course this includes several sizes of the same pattern. Nevertheless, never be at a loss to try the dressing for some recommended fly even though you have not got all the correct materials for the purpose. If pheasant is asked for, some other speckled type such as partridge or brown leghorn hen or cockerel will be good enough and might prove to be more attractive than the original type. By using a reasonable amount of substitutions one could be pleasantly surprised at the outcome.

Here are a few specifications of very successful flies:

March Brown – on hooks nos. 12, 14 or 16
Tail – light brown from pheasant, brown leghorn or partridge
Body – light brown wool or hare–lug spun onto the silk
Wing – as for tail taking from 6 to 10 fibres depending on the size of hook. Silk fawn or nearest.
Hackle – ginger brown from leghorn cockerel or nearest.

Note: to spin the hare–lug on to the silk, wet the fingers, take a few fur hairs from the lug and press them onto the silk next to the hook. Twist them round the silk and as the silk is wound round, keep adding tiny quantities of the hair, while dampening it the while, with "spit" on the fingers. When sufficient of the hair covers the body, stop and take away any loose hair, put on the usual half–hitches and proceed to the wing or hackle as desired.

Grey Spider – Hook sizes as above
Tail – 2 or 4 long teal fibres

Body – Grey wool with narrow tensil well spaced
Hackle – grey minorcca cockerel or hen with extra turns.
Wing – nil
Silk – fawn or nearest

Bronze Coachman – On hooks 12 and 14
Tail – peacock harl with widely spaced bronze tinsel (medium)
Hackle – white or white dyed yellow
Wings – white hen or gull
Tinsel – Bronze – narrow well spaced

Teal and Blue
Tail – 2 fibres of Jungle-Cock Fowl or pheasant ruff (neck)
Body – light-blue wool equally ribbed with narrow silver tinsel
Wing – teal duck – 12 to 16 fibres well "rolled".
   Note: To make a rolled wing, grip the fibres on the feather and push them forward so that they are straight out from the quill, – i.e. at right angles – keeping them in position so that all the thicker ends are together. Roll them between the fingers into a roll and fix them on top of the body.
Hackle – dyed white cockerel to a light blue.
Silk – light blue or white.
   For Teal and Red, Teal and Yellow, Teal and Green change the colour of the wool and the hackle to suit. All will have silver tinsel except for the yellow which should have gold tinsel.

Cinnamon and Gold – hooks usually 12 and 14
Tail – 4 to 6 fibres from Rhode Island hen wing.
Body – gold tinsel only, solidly covering hook.
Wing – as for tail, but the curve of the fibres back to back.
Hackle – ginger or fawn.
Silk – fawn or brown

Woodcock and Yellow – hooks 14 or 16 – smaller than the others.
Tail – 2 fibres of Jungle-cock or from pheasant "ruff".
Body – Hare-lug spun on followed with clear nylon rib.

Hackle – white cockerel dyed yellow.
Wing – attempt to have wings of identical design on each feather and fix one on each side, not on top.
Silk – yellow or white.

Bloody Butcher – hooks 12 and 14. Compare with silver butcher.
Tail – from dyed red – 4 to 6 fibres
Body – Red wool with narrow gold tinsel widely spaced.
Hackle – white cockerel dyed red.
Wing – 10 to 12 fibres of true black–blackbird or crow
Silk – Red

Alexandra – hooks 12 or 14
Tail – 4 fibres of strong black crow or cockerel wing.
Body – peacock harl closely wound all the way.
Wing – 3 to 6 short cuttings of peacock harl (rolled) in threes or all together.
Hackle – Black minorcca cockerel with brown or red sparkle.
Silk – black or green.

Grouse and Claret – Hooks 10, 12 or 14
Tail – Jungle-cock or from pheasant ruff
Body – Claret or maroon wool, well picked out and widely spaced narrow gold tinsel.
Hackle – brown leghorn cockerel or dyed nigger-brown.
Wing – from wing or tail of grouse, well balanced in design.
Silk – claret or dark red.

Greenwell's Glory This fly can be produced in all sized from 18 up to 6 and several different materials can be used in its make up. As long as the solid gold body and the ginger tackle is used and the wing is light brown or blue, it will catch fish. Hooks 6 to 18.
Tail – nil
Body – solid gold tinsel or other gold material such as stripes from Christmas parcel-wrapping or from stout chocolate wrapping. Some sportsmen put on yellow wool and gold tinsel with very little space between.
Hackle – ginger or nearest – keep to ginger if possible.

Elements of Angling

Wing – blae–blue or dark part of pigeon wing.
Silk – light brown, or yellow. (to go with ginger hackle)

This is not by any means the complete list of flies which I have used but they feature prominently in the part of my records which have noted successes. And now below is a list of flies which have become my favourites when fishing for seatrout:

Black Spider, Wickam's Fancy, Silver Butcher, Woodcock and *Hare Lug, Greenwell's Glory* (smallish sizes).

Dry Flies: *Blue Bottle, Iron Blue Dun, Tup's Indispensible, Bronze Coachman* (in small sizes) *Pale Olive* and *Blackgnat.*

There is little need to use a larger number until more experience has been gained, when more varied types can be tried out and added to your repertoire once you have judged their worth to your own particular type of fishing which could vary according to where you fish – loch or stream, reservoir or gently flowing river.

Some salmon flies: I have gone to extremes in experimenting with flies suitable for taking salmon and the times spent in studying the habits of young salmo, fry, parrs and smolts have been well worth while. For all that, I have come to the conclusion that really the salmon must be in the mood to take, and that there is no one type of fly which will guarantee success. When I recall some of the musty and half eaten types of flies that have taken salmon, I sometimes wonder if there is any need to put a dressing on them. It is all very well stating this, but that will not help very much, so here is a list of my favourite salmon flies, including the specifications for two flies of my own make up which are designed in keeping with my observations of the smaller flies which attracted parr and smolts while fishing for trout or seatrout:

List: *Jock Scott, Thunder and Lightning, Cape Goose, Brown Turkey, Silver Doctor, The Shrimp,* and *the Stoat's Tail,* and my own two designs which I call *Merry Widow* and *Black Magic*

Black Magic – Hooks No. 8, 9 or 10
Tail – white hen dyed yellow 4, 6, 8 fibres depending on the size of hook.
Body – Abdomen yellow or orange wool thorax red wool, all with

Elements of Angling

    broad gold or bronze tinsel as ribbing, spaced one and a half times the breadth of the tinsel and the wool well picked out between the ribbing)
Hackle – white cockerel dyed yellow or orange and followed by black with red or brown lustre.
Wing – Black from crow or other type with underlay of 6 to 8 fibres of yellow on top of white dyed red 4 to 6 fibres according to size of hook.
Silk – yellow or orange and finish with orange sealing wax to form head.

Merry Widow – Similar size of hooks

Tail – strong black 4 to 6 strands.
Body – green wool with equally spaced medium gold tinsel
Hackle – very soft white hen dyed light green and a good quantity of it.
Wing – Black crow as hood, over underlay of teal or mullard 6 to 8 strands on top of a similar amount of green.
Silk – emerald green and finish with green wax as head.

    Salmon and large seatrout have fallen to both flies during dusk and even later. The *Merry Widow* has accounted for three during bright sunshine according to my note book.

Casting with the fly

    By watching an expert caster with a well balanced rod and line, an observant tyro will learn more about casting than from any amount of written instruction. I myself derive a great deal of pleasure from watching an angler of experience handling good equipment with perfect grace, harmony and power to cause his flight of flies to alight gently on to the water's surface as daintily as airborne thistle down. This is an achievement seldom accomplished in a short period of time. It requires a great degree of patience, determination and skill. "Make haste slowly", is the order of the day. For what the written instruction is worth, study the drawings on page **47**. This should give a good understanding of the principles involved. If desired, the first attempts could be made away from the water. The rod will have line and cast attached but no fly and practice can be done on a lawn, in a field or play–

Elements of Angling

ground which is not too rough on surface to damage the line.

Casting by Numbers

When the rod is set up, draw from 3 to 4 metres of cast and line through the rod ring. Step back so that the line stretches out in front and proceed as follows:

(1) *Lift up the extended rod to tighten the line and pretend that you are making sure that the lure is not snagged or in a fish – count one to yourself for that part.*

(2) *Count two as you pull the rod smartly up and back, gently at first, and then gradually with increasing force and speed until the rod goes beyond the vertical.*

(3) *After pausing for an instant to allow the line and cast time to go back and count three as the forward cast is made, gently at first and gradually increasing the forward thrust until the rod is pointing towards the "point of entry", i.e. that part of the "water" where you wish the cast to alight. Hold this position for a second or two as the cast swings round and follows round giving slight movements to the line as it comes further round in the current. Hold a few seconds at the end of the cast as it may have been followed by a fish.*

Keep practicing while observing any faults and attempting to rectify them. Keep saying the numbers aloud or to yourself – (1) (2) *pause* **and (3) each time the complete cast is attempted.**

Striking your Fish

From the instruction given in bait fishing it may appear that striking your fish is an easy part of angling. This is far from the case. To those, who acquire this early in their angling career I would say that they have been fortunate, for there are many who do not do this well after years of angling. After all, it is for this very chance to strike your fish that you have been casting your flies upon the water. So give this section of angling a great deal of respect, time, thought and concentration, for the trout or salmon is in a more drastic position than the angler. On the occasion of a strike, a fish takes a lure and only has a fraction of a second to realise it has made a mistake and if it does not remedy the mistake in that fraction of a second it is usually hooked to meet its end. At the other end of the line the angler has the same fraction of a second to solidly hook the fish although if he makes a mistake the consequences are not so serious for him. He lives on and could easily be able to have a go at the same fish again.

Elements of Angling

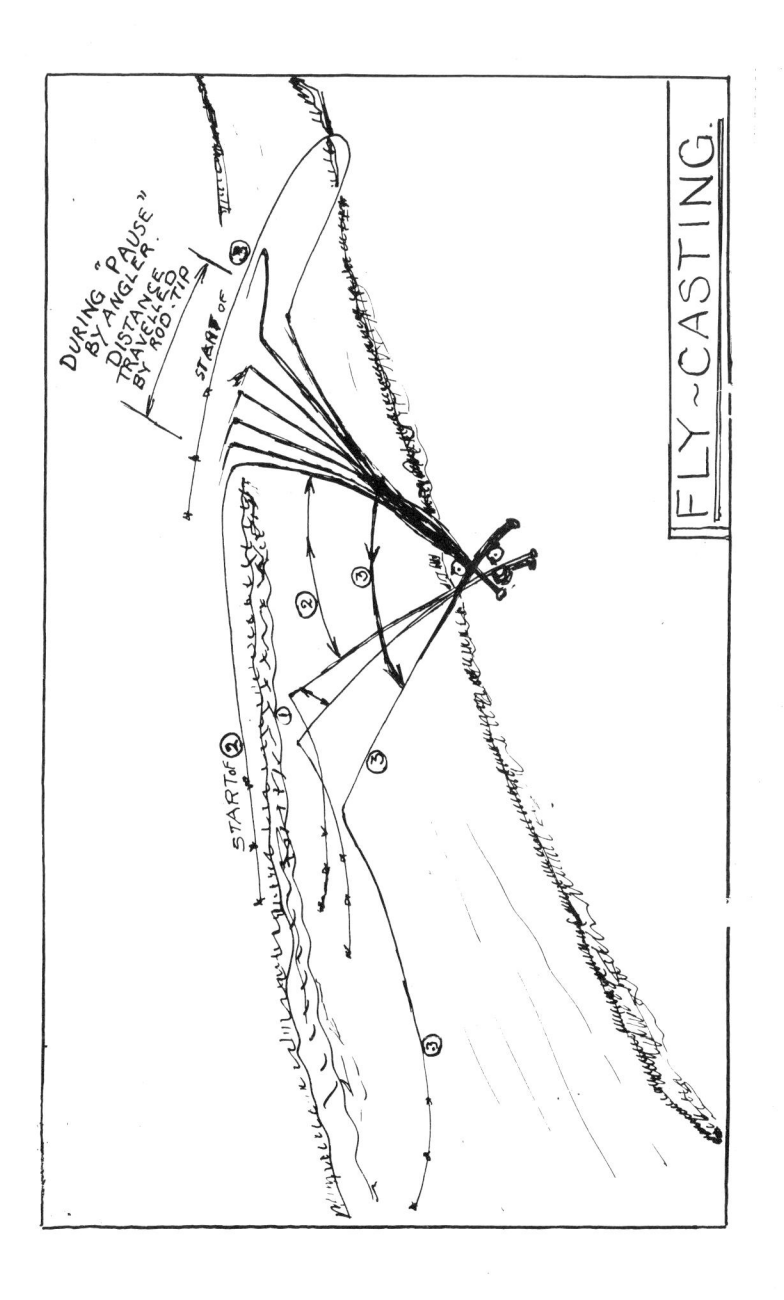

Figure 3.11 Fly Casting

Elements of Angling

It is true that success breeds success, for once the striking becomes more frequently successful, the attentive angler comes to know how his success comes about. It will soon be evident that concentration is the keynote to hooking a big percentage of rising fish. On a day when fish are reluctant to rise, the tendency is to allow the concentration to drop and sure enough when a rise does take place, the reactions are usually just that little bit slower. I myself am often caught out in this way. I sometimes allow my thoughts to wander as I near the end of a pool by anticipating how I might approach the next pool and, sure enough, the big one is missed! Similarly, while fishing the last few casts in a smooth deep run, the mind is allowed to dream thus:

"*The last time I was on the next pool I rose a big fellow in the far corner – I must not miss it, if it rises when I cover him this time*"

and, as you become that little bit less alert, another good sized fish takes your fly but ejects it again before you can take control. If you fail to strike the chance is gone.

In Figure 3.12 are three different methods of striking, but do not assume that these are the only methods. Some advocate not striking at all, while others are really ferocious in hooking a fish. The three methods given here have all gained contact with a high percentage of rising fish. A friend of mine was a great believer in striking "on" or "off" the reel with much success until one time he broke his rod. I know another who did most of his fishing on still water (lochs and reservoirs) and who waited until the fish had turned away sideways at which point he counted two seconds and gently lifted the rod usually with the fish on.

(A), (B) and (C) are the illustrations of the methods which I prefer. (A) is the fast strike in the direction shown away from the fish, the strike used by most fishermen, that is, the normal strike. (B) is a slow but deliberate ease off on the line followed by a firm hold up stream, making contact and then taking control. (C) is what is called the "push-strike" - in other words a quick jerk towards the fish immediately it rises or is felt. It may be a surprise to many seasoned anglers to learn that this action actually pulls very quickly on the hook and an instant touch means instant hooking.

In method (A) examine the action of the rod carefully, number (1) being the starting point. (2) is the first movement of the rod tip and (3) is the ultimate position of the rod-tip after the strike has been completed. Similarly with (B) and (C) a series of simple experiments can be carried out to prove that the rod behaves as indicated under the stipulated forces. They are as follows:

With the rod reel, line and cast in place hold the rod in a horizontal position so that the tip of the rod is from three to four inches above a table or some other suitable object. Give a sudden pull upwards on the rod and note

Elements of Angling

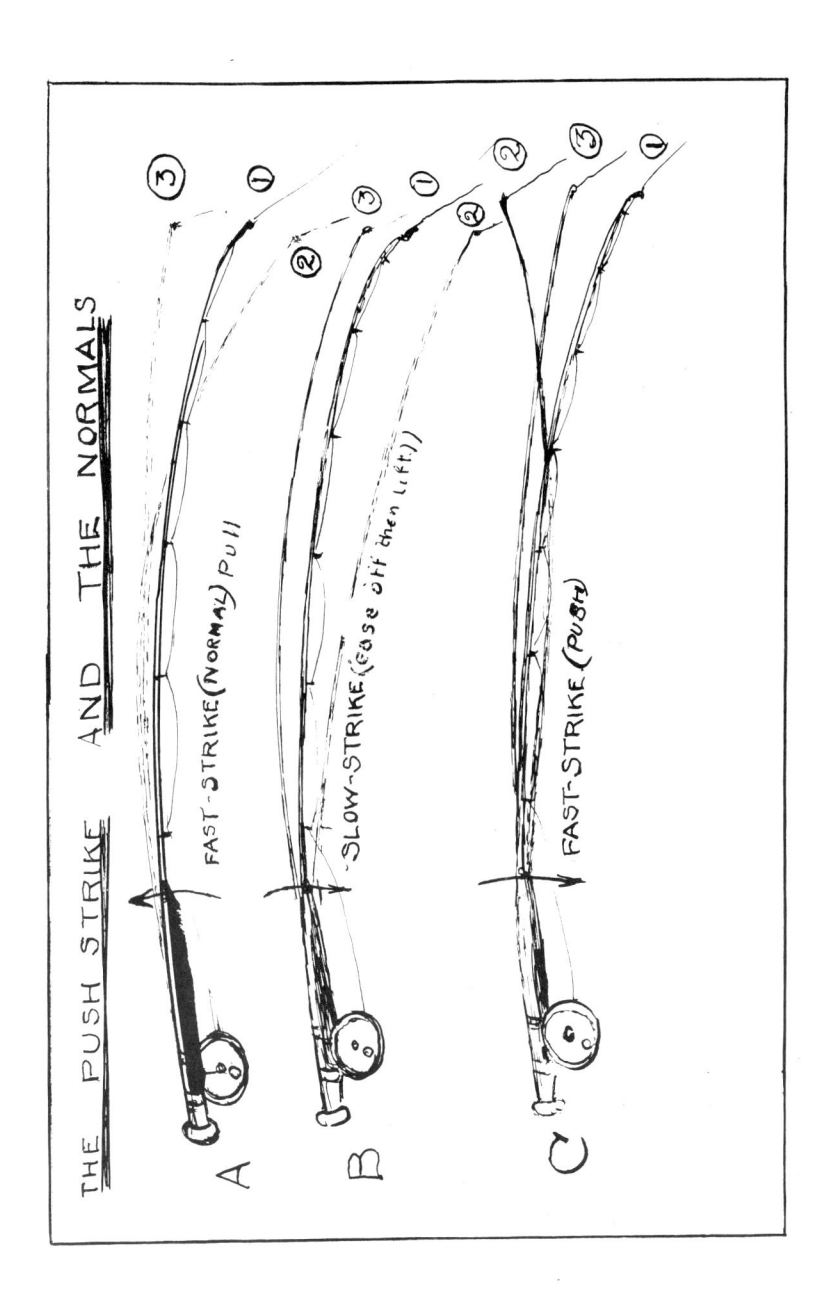

Figure 3.12 The Push (Fast) Strike and the Normal

what happens. The rod will flex in the direction of the pull to a little beyond its middle, but from there upwards it will flex in the opposite direction and the tip will actually strike down on the table. Now try the opposite. Hold the rod near a shelf or, even better, under the branch of a tree. It will be found that if the rod is pushed smartly away from the branch, it will hit it before following in the direction of the push. This type of cast first proved successful while I was attempting to overcome the difficulty of a dead calm when fishing on Camphill Dam (Paisley Waterworks). The technique was to keep casting gently where fish were seen so that when a fish rose within casting distance it was covered as soon as possible before the rings had gone. I would recommend that young anglers should become proficient at several methods of striking as it is difficult to change later. I would like to be present when a well-seasoned angler, who has been accustomed to striking off the reel, tries to master the push-strike as, four times out of five, when a fish rises he will strike from the reel. So be familiar with several methods of striking and apply them individually to suit conditions and other special circumstances.

Playing and Landing Your Fish

One of the biggest disappointments which can be experienced by any angler is to fish all day and, during the last few minutes of the alloted fishing spell, to hook a good fish, the best rise of the day, only to find that the line, cast, knot, or lure was faulty all along and gave up immediately contact was made. Seldom can he blame any one but himself. He has neglected to test his tackle from time to time. After he has changed a cast or replaced a fly, he should check over the changes made and at the same time take the opportunity to check all joins and knots by giving each a strong pull, while not neglecting the end of the line itself. Better to have a break then, than one when a good sized fish has been hooked, when he will lose both fish and tackle. There have been instances when the angler was not to blame and there will be a long queue of anglers all ready to tell you how they were let down by the failure of good new tackle. I do know of one individual, who had just fixed on a blue and silver devon and I witnessed him give the correct kind of tug as a test of his tackle's reliability. He fished for a short time and hooked a substantial salmon which he played for about five minutes under considerable strain. It lay down some distance away and the excited angler tried to get it moving again by going down stream and giving a little extra strain. Great was our astonishment when the line went slack and on winding in and examining the tackle, it was discovered that one of the hooks of the treble had

Elements of Angling

broken off. On further testing the other two hooks of the treble broke away under a comparatively mild strain on the 6 B.S. nylon. It was concluded that the hooks were not correctly tempered and therefore the fault must be attributed to the hook-maker; and manufacturer. However, why did the hook not break off when it was tested is still a mystery. Few would think to test a hook.

Provided, then, that you have been constantly testing the tackle and, that you have been fortunate to contact a comparatively large fish, the first reaction is usually to hold on tightly, although this can cause a break due to the fish's very strong run. The line should be allowed to run but slightly restrained by pressure on the line with the reel check or with the finger on the fly line. When the run is nearing its end the rod should be quickly lifted high and at right-angles so that the curve of the rod will begin to absorb the strain. Attempts should be made to keep in touch with the fish at all times except when the tethered fish attempts to get away by rising out of the water altogether, when the strain should be eased off. The sudden re-entry into the water puts extra force on the cast if it is held too tightly. Do not expect every fish to follow the same pattern of behaviour – some will not come out of the water even through a very long fight. Some will twist and twirl round, while others will bore down deeply and a few might lie still as if they had collapsed and the angler may be deceived into thinking that he has been snagged. Others still will follow an unpredictable mixture of all these moves. The angler will learn from experience how to counter many of the moves of a fighting fish, but to prevent him from taking a longer time to gain this experience, here are a few general rules to follow, which should be helpful. It should, however, be borne in mind that the full gambit of a hooked fish's behaviour is not known even to the most *compleat angler*, for like every angler every fish will follow its own particular pattern of behaviour when in contact with rod and line. Let me revise:

1. As stated, allow the fish to have a good run on the check of the reel. Slow it gradually by putting on an increasing curvature on the rod and at the same time press lightly on the line at the butt or on the rim of the reel. If you are using a spinning reel the tension should be light at first and as the fight goes on it should be tightened gradually. It should never be so tight that the line breaks, nor so slack that it causes a tangle, a fankle, or a "bird's nest" because the time spent trying to untangle it may allow the fish to regain its freedom.

Should the fish attempt to descend to rapids below a pool, before you try to restrain it and risk a break, make sure that you could follow it downstream and that there are no trees or other obstructions in your path to follow down. If however a tree is there having a thin trunk, the rod can be passed from one hand to the other or a companion may do it for you. You can then follow the fish. If this is not possible then attempt to keep the fish in the pool at the risk of a break. If extra straining fails to turn the fish, try tearing off several metres of line and let it go slack completely. When it has eased off sufficiently the fish may think it is free, might cease fighting and may wish to return to the point in the pool where it was in the beginning.

2. Gently take up the line again. Try now to keep below it during the rest of the fight. If it cannot be kept in the pool and you can't follow it, try to get it to settle further down and get out the whistle which you should carry for just such an emergency in the hope that a fellow angler will come to your assistance.

3. If the fish rushes up past the neck of the pool and continues up the stream above, let him go. The further he travels in that direction the sooner he will tire and when the time comes to bring him back down, this should be done with a steady light strain. At the same time try to bring him closer to your own bank because, being shallower water, there is the possibility of becoming snagged on a boulder or some other object. If he is still "dour to fetch", go up the bank to a point directly opposite and put on a medium constant side strain with the rod well down, with the top almost touching the water. This will gradually tire the fish, but be alert for a sudden dart on the part of the fish, when you should be ready to give him his head once more.

4. There might come a time when you could feel the movement of the fish as he swings his tail from side to side to keep his place in the current. If you can detect this from your translation of the changing strains, you can give a slight extra pull when you sense that the fish's head is angled towards you and the tail is in the away position. If this move is correctly executed the fish will be brought nearer by stages for the final move to the net.

5. Should the fish tend to rise completely out of the water, act as follows: When you have some tension on the line, try to drop the point of the rod immediately, because as the fish and cast hit the water on the way down, the force may be too great at point of impact and you could be parted.

6. Should the fish tend to keep below your level and refuses to be "fetched" by any of the usual means, then try "pumping" him. To do this, lower the rod as you gently wind in some line and then with a little more force cause the fish to follow by slowly lifting the rod. Keep repeating this movement. The fish usually follows quietly, especially if his first mad rushes are over. If this fails, try walking up the bank with rod held high keeping it steady, especially if the fight is nearing an end. This is almost a "never-fail-method" but should be used as a last resort, because if he is not ready for the

net he may have a final fling for freedom.

If the fish is very large do not play it completely to the stage that it is floating tummy up. If you are near a strong current on your own side of the water or immediately above some streams and you are not able to follow down, as soon as it begins to show its white, try to bring it to the net as quickly as possible, because the "dead-weight" of a played-out fish is far more difficult to control and it soon becomes "out of hand". If it does reach the stricter water, the chances of keeping him becomes very slim indeed unless you have some one to help you.

Landing

When the fish is ready for the net, hold it steady at the bank edge and slip the net under it. Slowly relax the strain on the rod as you lift with the net and carry it well back from the bank. If the fish is large gently lay your rod down immediately after netting it and take control of the net with both hands. If a gaff or tailer is waiting, do not relax the strain on the rod one iota; if using a gaff, place it in the water. Hold it steady, bring the fish slowly up and over the upturned point of the gaff, pull up and out in one movement and do not stop until you are a reasonable distance from the bank so that the fish cannot slither back in again. If a tailer, try to steady the fish so that the tailer can be slipped over the tail and when opposite the "wrist" pull sharply up and take it away from the bank as before. The tailer is definitely less liable to loose a fish once it is tailed. Fish have got away after having reached the bank and if it has been gaffed and then gained its freedom there is no guarantee that it would survive such treatment. Where there are "kelts" about, do not use the gaff. Better to tail them out by hand, and if it is a kelt then you will do less harm. Remember to wet your hands before you handle such fish.

If you are taking part in a competition, place your catch in a plastic bag or along with grass in your creel because if the competition lasts, as it usually does, for a good number of hours then the evaporation due to an exceedingly hot day can be considerable. A warm day can cause a loss of weight. At competition time some keen anglers have been known to be very rough with smolts, salmon-parr and young trout not yet taking size. This is done only then, by some, because they do not want to waste time doing this while others may be lifting out one of the correct type and size. However, to all good anglers this seems terrible – it is the better angler who takes his time in this even though he may never win a prize. There is an idea that has got around that you should take the grip of the eye of a fly hook when a parr is on it, between your finger and thumb, and the fish will shake itself off. I have seen a fish drop off in this way alright, except that it had left one lip behind; that is, the maxillary (see Figure 9.1).

Elements of Angling

Figure 3.13 A 7lbs. 1oz. fish taken on fly; the Merry Widow, No. 8 hook at Pow's Dam
Water was almost run off after a spate 11.-10 am

Elements of Angling

Figure 3.14 River Doon, Pow's Dam, Near Dalrymple

Patches of blue sky were showing through a white cloud covering and thlight south-westerly breeze on the last Saturday of the 1955 season when "Black Magic" a newly designed salmon fly got to grips with this 20 pounder and within about half-an-hour brought it to the net of the writer. The river was low but there was ample water to add zest to the fight around 4.30pm

Elements of Angling

The best way I know is to dangle the small fish on the line in such a way that it is still held up by the water and on the surface. With the rod held steady almost upright, reach down with the other hand. Wet the hand in the water and lift it out, putting down the rod. Wet the other hand and carefully remove the hook. If difficult, use some form of disgorger and slip the fish back into the water and hope that it will recover.

There are too many ways already which deplete the fishing stocks without injuring the young fry in this way. It is up to all concerned to see that the small fry are returned to the water in sound and healthy condition.

The wetting of the hands helps to prevent the fish scales from being removed. To bare the skin of the fish to the dangers of some of the dreaded diseases that abound in some waters today is a very real danger.

SALMON AND FISHERIES ACTS

The conviction and fining of so many poachers relating to the illegal taking and possession of salmon and other fresh water fish has stimulated the vast angling fraternity to seek further information. It is not within the scope of a feature of this dimension to go into every aspect of all the fishery laws that apply, but herewith is a summary of the salient points, that should help the average angler to assess the significance of the proposed fines relating to the many offences for which the mode of prosecution may be summarily fixed on indictment. The details are taken from *The Freshwater Fish (Scotland) Act* 1902; *The Trout (Scotland) Act* 1933; *The Salmon and Freshwater Fisheries (Protection) (Scotland)* Act 1951 and *Freshwater and Salmon Fisheries (Scotland) Act* 1976.

Type of Offence	Penalty for 1st Offence	Penalty for 2nd Offence
Fishing without a permit	£50	£100
Fishing by illegal means	£100	£200
Illegal fishing by two or more acting together	3 months or £200	6 months or £400
Use of explosives, poisons and electrical devices	3 months or £200	6 months or £400
Unauthorised removal of dead fish	£100	£200

Elements of Angling

Type of Offence	Penalty for 1st Offence	Penalty for 2nd Offence
Obstruction of Water Bailiff, Constable, etc.	3 months and/or £100	3 months and/or £100
Fishing for Salmon on Sundays	£100	£200
Refusing or neglecting to provide statistics	£100	£100
Fishing for Salmon by rod and line during close-season contrary to by-law provision	£50	£100
Prevent the passage or catching fish at fish-passes	£100	£200
Contravention of any by-law (on fishing) not specified	£100	£200
Buying, selling or possessing salmon roe	£50	£100
Buying, selling, taking or possessing unclean or unseasonable salmon or salmon taken in close-season	£50	£100
Fishing for or possessing trout during close-season or purchase or sale of trout under 8 inches	£50	£100

Elements of Angling

Figure 3.15 Youthful Enthusiasm

PART 2
SPINNING
&
SPINNING LURES

4

AN INTRODUCTION TO THE SPINNING ROD

The prospect of taking spinning as a correct sequence of events may not be in agreement with common opinion, but from my observations, I have found that beginners, especially young beginners, have become more proficient with a spinning rod than with the longer salmon fly rod. This may be due to the fact that large trout, seatrout and salmon can be taken often while using spinning lures.

No reference is made at this time to the types of spinning equipment which can be bought nor to their trustworthiness. This should be reserved for the future when the tyro has had some experience. The only words of advice which can be passed on meantime is that the beginner should not go in for the most expensive rods and reels to be had, not until he is able to make up his mind whether he will be a bait, or fly enthusiast or will spend most of his fishing time spinning. It is recommended that to make a start he should obtain a reasonably priced reel and a rod about 2 metres long, with the spool filled with monofilament nylon about 8 or 10 B.S. Do not use much heavier nylon, which is thicker and stiffer and is liable to spring off the spool. If allowed to go slack, it can cause a serious tangle – known in the sport as a "bird's nest" which can take some time to sort out, trying the patience of the most forebearing person.

I recall a young aspirant who was given a grandiosian spinning reel, which had everything added to make it perfectly fool-proof. It was so complicated that he was always in trouble at the riverside. He tended to become the laughing stock of all the other youths, so much so that in the end he gave up completely and has not been seen at the butt end of a rod since. Such a gift so early in a fishing career is far from kindness. It can possibly result in the loss of a potential sportsman. Extricating oneself from the devilish tantrums of a "bird's nest" can be very trying once in a day, but to have this happen repeatedly very soon loses the frivolity of a joke and especially if it happens just as you strike a fish, which actually happened to the fellow

Elements of Angling

referred to.

When you have furnished yourself with the requisite equipment – a spinning-rod, a simple but sturdy spinning-reel and a spool well filled with nylon of about 10 B.S. go out to some open space and, with a 2.50 " wire nail or woodscrew or other object of similar weight attached to represent the lure, such as an artificial minnow, let the business of casting begin. Keep well away from windows or other breakables including other practicing anglers because in the beginning many mis-timed casts "get away". Take any safety precautions that can be anticipated. See also that no animals are within range in any direction.

Casting the Side-Swing

With the rod held at about 45° facing supposedly down stream and with the rod pointing in the same direction – swing the body round as if on a pivot, gripping the line tightly against the butt with the forefinger. Allow the casting arm to come back and behind you. Pause to give the lure time to come back a little further and with a swinging movement, thrust the rod forward with a gradually increasing force and finish with the rod pointing almost directly opposite to you as far out as you can. The entry point can be an imaginary point across a lawn or far out in a field. As the movement is about to be completed, release the forefinger on the butt and the lure should spin out to the end of the cast. Now, with the other hand, which should be at the ready position, turn the handle to engage the pick-up. Imagine you are fishing and wind in the line slowly. Repeat the casting until you feel that you are mastering this efficiently. Should you mis-time the release, one of two things will take place. If you release the grip too soon the lure will fall beside you at your feet on the bank or in the water close to you. If on the other hand you are too late in releasing the finger, then the "lure" will in all probability make a threatening circle under the rod and if too much line was out to start with, you could easily find the lure striking your leg or other part of your anatomy or perhaps some other person's anatomy. This shows that while casting in this way the line which was taken out before the cast is made, should be slightly less than that which would reach the hands at the butt.

When you are satisfied that your efforts on "dry land" are of such proficiency that you can strike a cardboard fish say three times out of four then go to the water and have a turn in earnest.

To retrieve the lure correctly you must now study the pool or stream in detail. I would recommend that spinning in shallow streams should not be attempted until a month or two has been put in at spinning in deeper water. Determine where the fastest currents are – where the lies for fish are located and fish your lure fast or slow to suit and also try to keep the lure at the desired

Elements of Angling

depth by raising or lowering the rod tip. There is a wonderful knack in this, which can best be gained by watching others and by experimentation. There is a wealth of hints and know how in Alexander Wanless's Book on *Thread-Line Fishing* but the angler's own experience is best of all.

Over-head Casting

Some call this distance-casting. Where there is ample head room and where extra distance might get results, this is the cast to use. For this cast a little less line need be hanging from the rod. The rod is held very much higher and by means of a more forceful swing to the rear without turning the body as last time and with an upward force to an overhead movement, impart a very forceful thrust forward so that the lure goes quite high in the air. Thus it will get a much further projectile flight to the point of entry. If satisfactorily carried out it is amazing how far the lure can be flighted.

A Spinning Rod is sometimes used from a Boat.

The best results are usually obtained by trawling. Two rods are set at the two corners of the boat stern and point outwards away from one another. Considerable length of line is drawn from each and allowed to follow the boat at a considerable distance. The boat should be rowed at a moderate speed and in a zigzag fashion. One angler rows while the other takes charge of the rods, but if a fish is felt, rowing stops immediately. The rods are kept apart until the rower can take charge of his own rod either with the fish on that line, or if on the other, he will wind in his line to prevent a tangle of the two lines taking place and make the netting of the fish much easier.

When spinning on still waters, be it loch or river, it pays to vary the speed and depth of the lure but when spinning in streams the varying currents may be sufficient variation without extra from the fisher. In truth, while fishing streams the actual retrieving can be suspended completely for a good part of the cast. Especially can this be done in the strongest currents and immediately the lure comes out of the fastest part of the current retrieving should be recommenced quickly. Retrieving too slowly in both pool or stream will be sure to lose lures and tackle.

Summing up - the correct cast should take your lure , say , from two to three metres above and little less, beyond where you think fish are lying, and to do this, stand directly opposite the point of entry and to be accurate in this, bring the pick-up into action as the lure reaches the point of entry.

Elements of Angling

Spinning lures

There are many types of lures used by the angler who has become a regular spinner. Minnows, natural and artificial, pickled prawns, spoons, plugs and other items of varied shapes, colours and sizes all find a place in the repertoire of this kind of angler; and there are fundamental subtitles in the methods of presenting them to the fish. Some are caused to rotate as they pass through the water. Artificial minnows have fins, wings or propellers which rotate the whole lure. Spoons are so constructed that only the spoon part rotates round a central body. Plugs and other related lures are made to wobble and dodge about irregularly like a wounded minnow. The lures, which rotate as a whole necessitate the use of swivels – one, two or three spaced along the cast. With heavy lures of this type the thin nylon line tends to twist and tangle and curl up to jam the reel. This can be minimised, if time is taken to change the minnow from one turning clockwise to one turning anti-clockwise. This, however, is time consuming and so an anti-kink device is recommended. At one time I used a lead washer, which I doubled over the nylon, but lead is no longer used in fishing, therefore I now obtain a thin piece of copper or brass about 25 by 12mm and clinch it over the nylon so that it hangs down, acting as a vane to retard the twisting tendency of the line and if correctly applied can stop the twisting altogether. Spoons and plugs do not require this refinement but spoons are less liable to snag than minnows because of their construction.

Home- made Artificial Minnows

There are many ways of obtaining home made minnows and it is now proposed to give some of the easier ways of making them. This is done not so much to economise, but to give the angler something to keep him interested during the closed season and this may help to keep him enthusiastic; for success with home made lures does add to the fun and success with them is very satisfying indeed. See Figure 4.2.

A short length of old electric cable is used. By means of two pairs of pliers, withdraw the internal wire leaving the outside casing. Take out the insulation: string wax and other materials as at (A) and (B). Make paxolin casing straight and perfectly round by inserting a thin dowel, large nail or some other suitable object and by forcing it through and tapping with a hard piece of wood used in the same way as a plumber's "dresser". It is now covered with plastic wood and shaped into the form of a minnow; a streamlined form. See portion not covered with plastic wood. This is left, so that (F) can be fitted into the hold at (O) when it is left to dry and set, otherwise, if left on the side, the plastic would finish flat on one side. Any accidental marks will require to be removed later, but while the drying is taking place it can be placed as shown at (F). When the final smoothing is completed it can also be placed

Elements of Angling

at (F) while it is being painted in the chosen colours. There are so many ways of painting – dark colour above and light colour below being the most popular colouring. colours from the full range of the spectrum are used – some showing stripes others with dots and eyes. Looking over ;my records I find that I have been fairly successful with artificial minnows about 1 3/4" painted dark green on the top and a light yellow belly.

In Figure 4.2 at letter (N) is shown another method of making a core. An old milk bottle top is washed and dried to prevent smell and is then carefully flattened out. An attempt should be made to prevent it from splitting apart at the edges. This is best done by slow manipulation between the fingers and using very little force. Take a piece of 1/8" dowel rod or other object and roll the milk top round it. At the middle it will be thicker but that will add to the form when the plastic wood surrounds it to form the body. The work from there on is exactly the same as for the last type.

When it is completed it will be found to be very much lighter than the first. So much so that if you were to attempt to fish with it, it would always float to the surface. It is therefore necessary to put on a fair weight. This can be combined with the need for an anti-kink device. Make it of heavier material or larger or add a second one. This can be adjusted at times so that the lure can be fished at different depths and this minnow usually fished at less depth than others can be expected to be snag-free. There is one drawback, however, when the anti-kind device is snagged the light minnow cannot be slid up the line, with the current, to free it.

Figure 4.1 From the Record Book.
Cassillis Stretch on the Doon on home made minnow lure $1^{3}/_{4}$" (Devon) one from Dubb's Pool 11 $^{1}/_{2}$ lbs. one from Keeper's Pool 8 $^{1}/_{4}$ lbs.

Elements of Angling

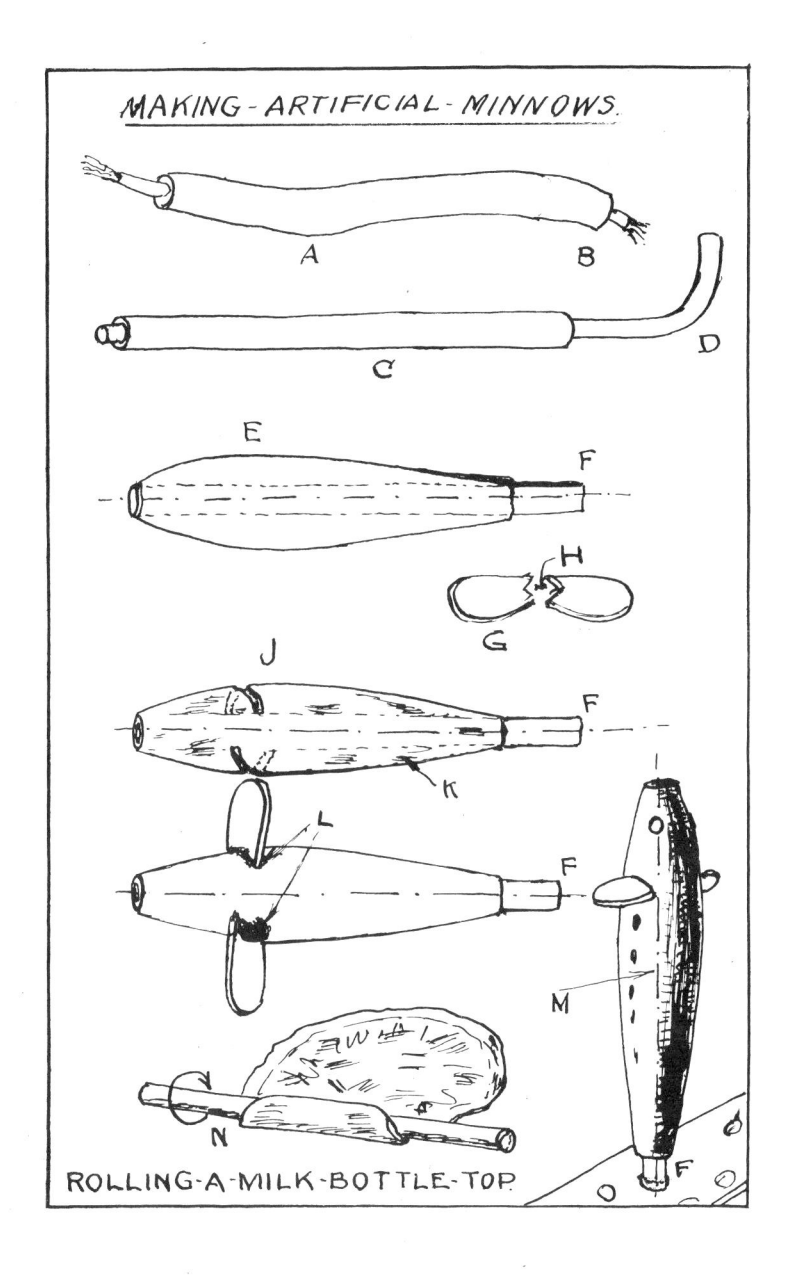

Figure 4. 2 Making Artificial Minnows

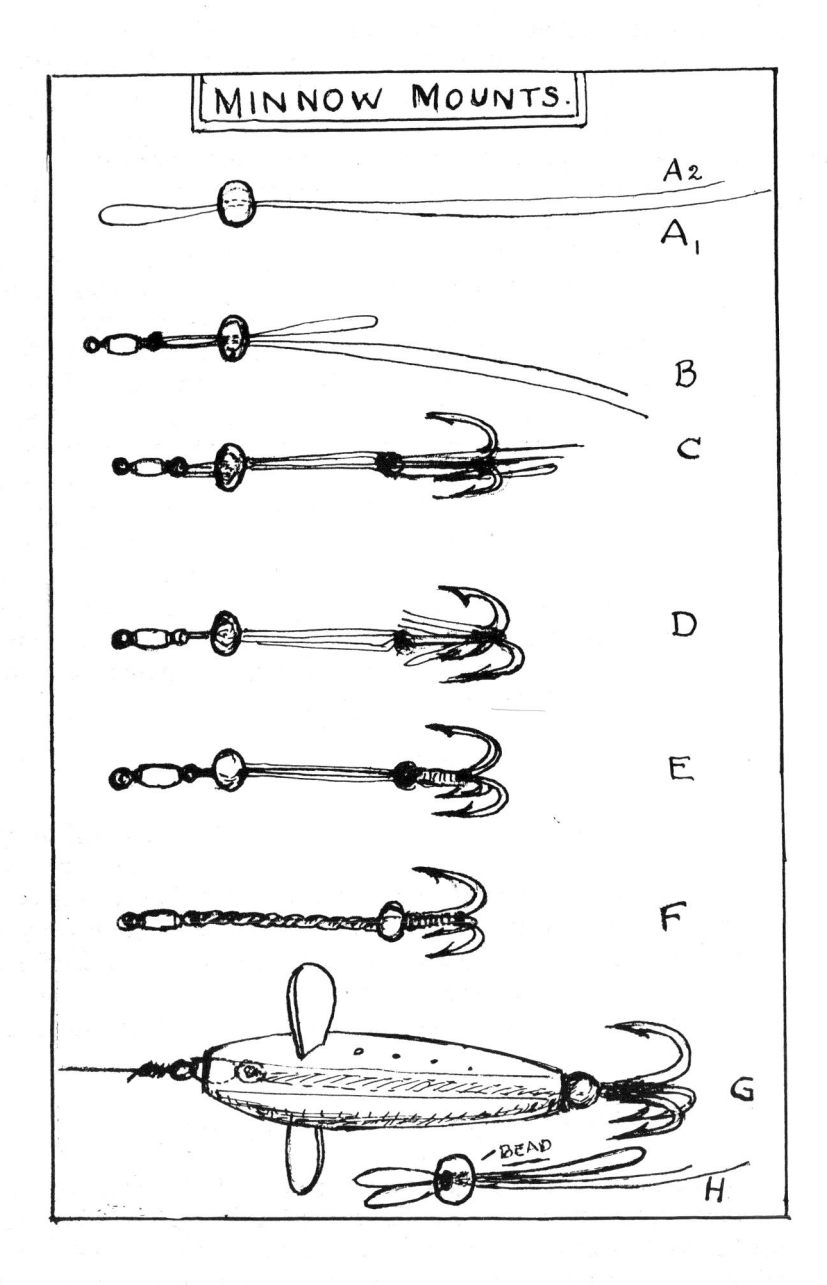

Figure 4.3 Making the Minnow Mount

Elements of Angling

The natural follow on after making a good looking artificial minnow is to make a mount to go with it. Illustration in Fig. 4.3 shows that this can be done by procuring a coil of trace wire "Elasticum" about 6 B.S. a treble hook of No. 12 or 10 size eyed preferred, a swivel of not more than 2 mm diameter to suit size indicated in the illustration and a bead around 4 mm. Beads used are usually red but can be of another colour. Success has been attained with white beads.

Cut off about half a metre of wire. Double fold it so that one end is about a centimetre longer than the other. See A1 and A2. This will help when trying to pass the folded wire through the bead then through the eye of the swivel as at (B) and back through the bead to (C) where it was passed through the eye of the hook then round the body and in between the hooks of the treble and then round the stem using up the remainder of the wire to clinch the end of the wire by winding the hook stem with brown or black silk thread. To make the full mount quite rigid the strands of wire between the swivel and the hook are twisted on one another. The whole mount should stay straight when held horizontal by the hook or the swivel. The mount should be of such a length that it has only the eye of the swivel protruding from the body of the minnow proper. If the swivel is inside the body there is every chance that the nylon cast can be cut with the inside edge of the minnow "mouth". For larger minnows extra strands of wire can be used with larger beads with larger holes in them to accommodate these extra strands.

Home Made Spoon

Here is another example of how an angler might keep himself occupied during the closed season. The spoon and particularly the type known as the Mepp has been popular for many years and still commands a great amount of attention because of its all round success in loch and stream. It has accounted for many trout, seatrout and salmon and in addition those who fish for pike get a creditable performance from its use.

This lure does not attempt to be a copy of any known creature, unless as one has said :

"It is taken for a small fish which has been injured."

No matter what is said about its origin or its identity with some form in nature it is a very effective lure. Size colour and design can vary considerably but the fundamental principle involved is the same. A piece of thin metal oval or pear shaped is dished and caused to rotate round the central body.

Elements of Angling

Figure 4.4 Salmon of 16lb. 9 oz.
**Caught on 2.25 in. home made minnow lure from Mirren's Pond .(Heavy waters ,
grey skies)**

Elements of Angling

Material required:

A thin piece of brass, copper or aluminium; a length of wire not thicker than 30 s.w.g. This can be obtained by stripping a length of over-head distribution electrical cable; a few coloured beads or a length of small metal tubing and a treble hook of suitable size and a few simple tools such as those required to make the flat minnow. As indicated in Figure 4.5, cut the thin metal to an oval shape at (A) and (C) Smooth the edges with emery-cloth and files. Drill a small hole, about 2mm near to the top end. Prepare a hollow in a piece of hard wood and with a rounded stake or a repousse hammer or round nosed mallet. Try to obtain a consistent curve. Although the dishing may not be very deep it may be sufficiently effective, see (B) and (D). At letter (E) is shown the follower or chaser as it is technically known, which is hit into the hollow to do the dishing. Another way is to fix a domed stake in a vice and shape the metal round it with a hide mallet. If during this process the metal becomes harder with the working and is more difficult to form, it should be annealed.

This is done by heating it to a dull red and allowing it to cool slowly. If, however, aluminium is being used, it should be rubbed over with soap, so that when the soap turns black it will be realised that it is heated sufficiently and allowed to cool as before. If the aluminium is not covered with soap, there will be no warning, that the metal is being over-heated until a portion of the metal drops off.

When this part is completed, take a piece of the wire and form an eye or loop as shown at (F) and with another piece of wire to make the staple clip as shown at (G). Round nosed pliers are preferred here. Note that the spoon part must be in place before the second twirl is put on. Take a much longer piece of wire than is necessary for ease of manipulation and the extra can be removed later. Also note that the short ends of the clip are **both** on the inside. This is so that the spoon will not be hindered in its turning. Pass the stem through the clip and put on three or four beads or a piece of metal tubing cut to length. Follow this with the treble hook. Judge the length so that the spoon just clears the hooks and bend the stem back then forward as at (M) then twist round itself at (K). The size (L) indicates the space to allow the wire to go round some two and a half times before it is cut and filed to give a flat end. Sometimes the space is made wider and a piece of red or orange coloured wool is added being fixed by tying silk of similar colour.

Note: It is recommended to keep the spoon highly polished on **both** sides. The glint of light reflected seems to be an added attraction especially for salmon. Do not use spoons made of aluminium in salt water. The surface soon becomes eroded and pitted and loses its lustre.

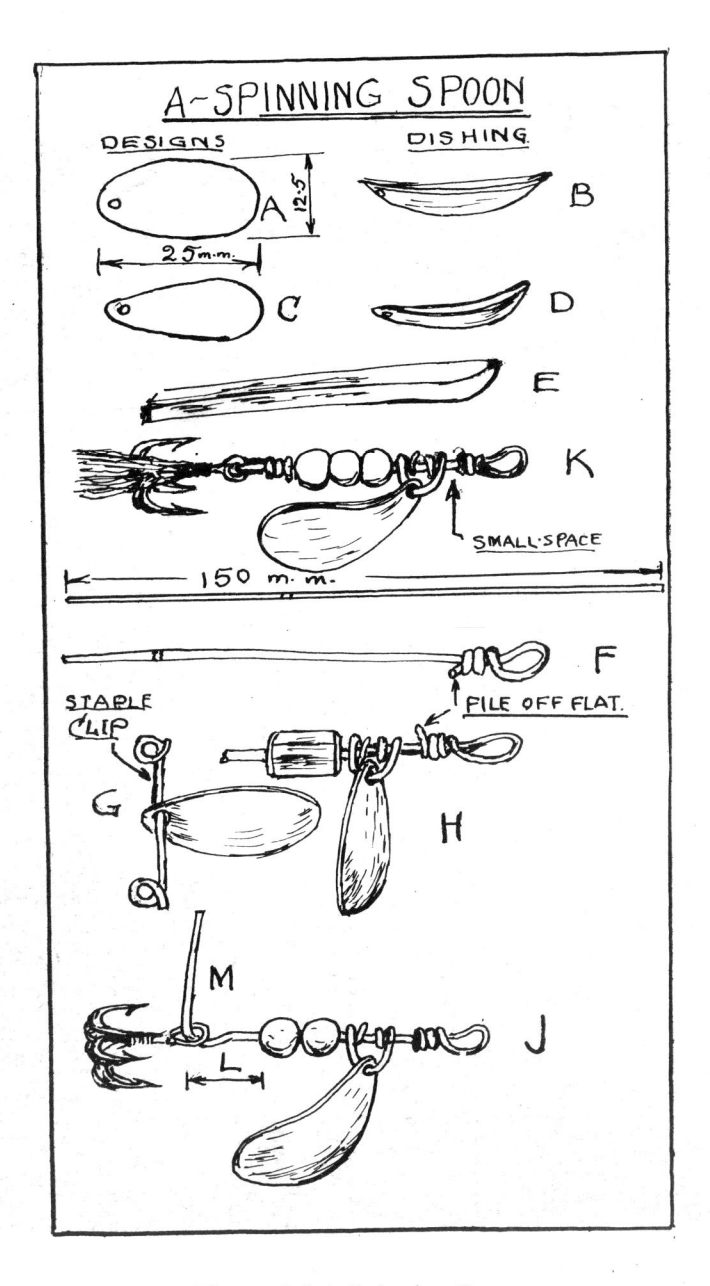

Figure 4.5 A Spinning Spoon

Elements of Angling

Figure 4.6   18 $^1/_2$ pounder on a 1 $^1/_4$" on Home Made Spoon

Elements of Angling

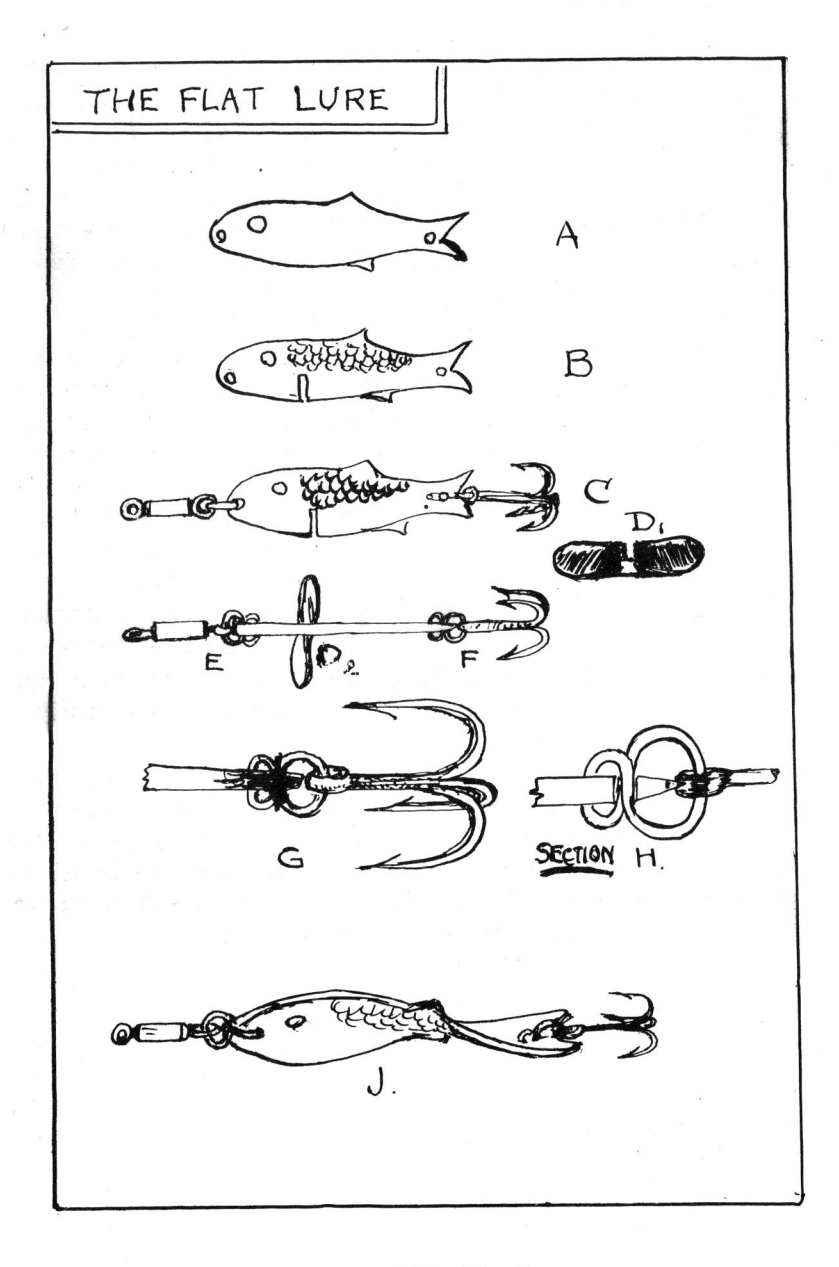

Figure 4.7 The Flat Lure

Elements of Angling

A Flat Minnow Lure: *See illustration in Fig. 4.7*

Obtain a piece of aluminium about 60mm long and 12.50 mm broad by 3 mm or 4 mm thick to make this attractive kind of lure. The tools required are, as for last lure, plus a hacksaw and a hand drill with a small bit. Scratch on the shape as shown at (A). Follow the scratched design with saw and finalise with file and emery. Round the edges and make it slightly thinner from the middle towards the tail. Drill a small hole at the nose and at the vee of the tail as near the end as possible but still leaving enough metal for strength. Drill only part way through to show eyes.

With the hacksaw cut the slot for the fins in the "tummy" about two fifths form the nose. This slot should be about 5mm deep and the metal for the fins should be exactly the thickness of the saw kerf. It should be remembered that for thinner metal a "Junior" hacksaw could be used for the slot.

The fins are now shaped as at (G) by twisting with the two pliers. When the fins are placed or forced into position they are keyed in by the punch hit on each side of the slot. If not considered firm enough use glue such as "araldite". It now remains to fix on the swivel and treble-hook in such a manner that the whole lure will take the strain of the "big one".

The finished article is shown at (E), while at (G) and (H) an attempt is made to show how two strands of wire pass through the hole in the body and how the ends of the wire are turned in against the body. Glue can be put at the hole but if desired to have more security thin trace wire an be wound round the crossing part of the wire at (G).

At (J) is shown how to cause the flat minnow to spin without fins. To do this, it is easier if thinner metal is used for the body? During construction or even after the lure is completed in the flat, take two pair of pliers and twist the body evenly all the way along. Both the above lures can be painted to suit the whims of the spinner, but results have been attained with the original colours of lures made from aluminium, copper or brass.

Figure 4.8 The River Stinchar from Pinwherry Bridge

PART 3

CONDITIONS – DRY FLY AND OTHER METHODS

5

DRY-FLY FISHING

Many anglers are of the opinion that dry-fly fishing is the finest known method of angling. Except for perhaps "dapping" I am inclined to agree. If you are in a position to try it correctly you will enjoy it immensely. On a day when the conditions will bring out the hatching flies on both loch and stream the best results can be obtained in water which is seldom more than a metre and not less than half a metre deep and especially in stretches of long runs which are comparatively fast running. Early dawn and late dusk are perhaps the preferred times. I delight in a summer evening when the heat of the day lingers and when the flies are on the wing particularly the May fly. Cloud cover is preferred although complete cloud cover is not essential. Bright sunshine directly on the water means conditions are more difficult if not nigh impossible. If it is really bright seek the shadows of the riverside growths.

On the illustration showing Dry-flies in the making, are the several commoner types used. In most cases the body is of the hairy type of natural fur, spun fur or of wool teaseled out after it is put on. Peacock or ostrich harl is sometimes used, put on in abundance so that there is ample fibre to hold some form of floatant and so that tiny air bubbles are trapped to help in the floatation of the hooked fly. Some enthusiasts recommend wide gap hooks, but I prefer very small hooks to save weight with a narrow gap so that the hook tends less to break the surface tension of the water. It may be that I do not hook so many fish out of the number of rises but that is more than compensated for by the increased number of rises? Therefore hooks seldom exceed No. 14 size. On occasion I have tried hooks as small as No. 24, but the grip on a hooked fish is so little that I gave up the practice and would not recommend using one so small.

Producing Dry-flies

To produce a good dry-fly commence as at (A) and put on a turkey or peacock harl tail; perhaps four fibres from the root of the hackle. Quite often

Elements of Angling

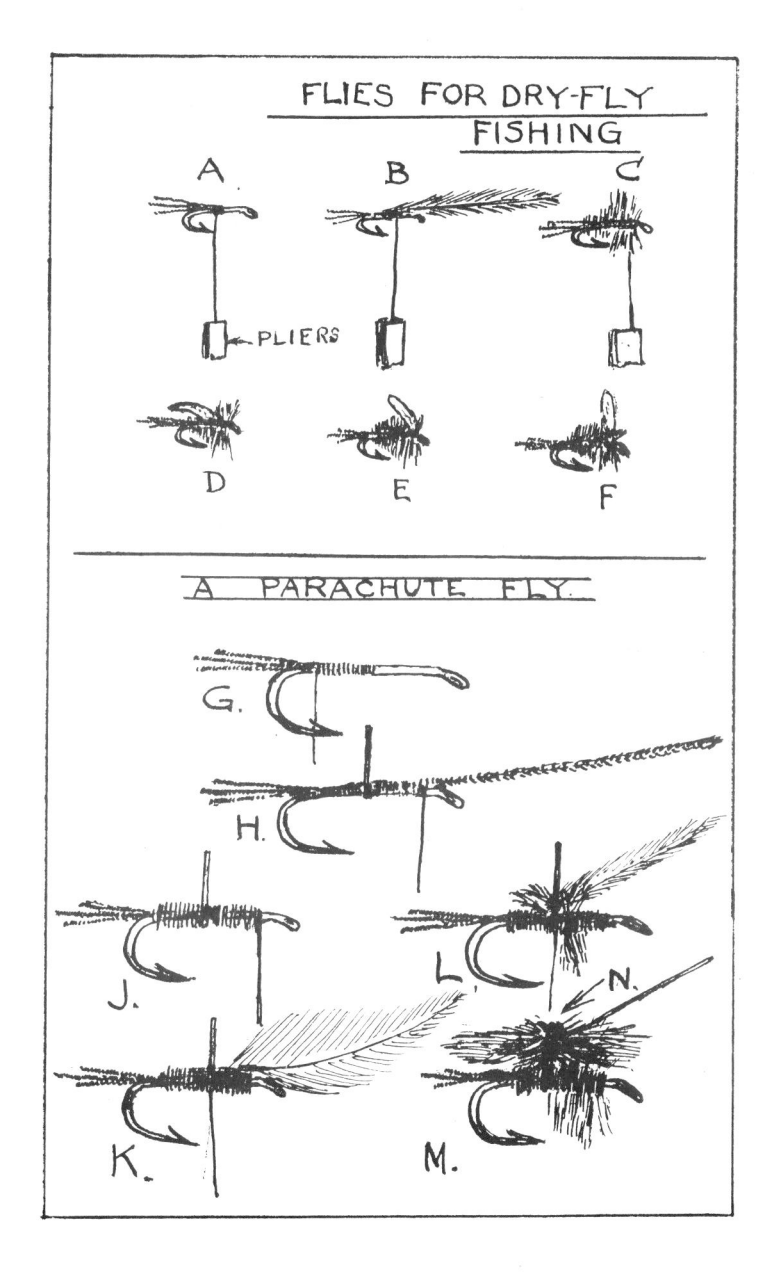

Figure 5.1 Flies for Dry–Fly Fishing

no tail is desired. Next take a medium sized hackle from stock to suit the fly which you have chosen, put it at the tail and wind it towards the head thus the longer fibres of the hackle will be at head. Lock the silk with half-hitches and pick out all trapped fibres as at (C). This could be used as dry-fly without any additional parts, however at (D), (E) and (F) are shown winged flies with the wings cocked at different angles. This is done by winding some of the silk behind the root of the wing to lift it up and hold it where desired. Try the slope of the wing as on a "Blae and Black" variety and with ample black hackle on the body and the wing in the position as at (D) it is surprising, when, once the finished fly is oiled, to see how like an ordinary house fly it will look. A friend of mine tried to make the likeness still more pronounced by tying in cellophane winds, but alas they were easily broken off. To counter this, he glued the cellophane to a feathered wing. This gave the same effect. The cellophane remained for a longer period but ultimately came off also.

In the lower portion of Figure 5.1 , about four times actual size,is shown a progressive method of obtaining an excellent dry-fly known as the parachute fly. This fly alights very lightly on the surface and will seldom break the boundary layer (surface tension) as it descends. (G) shows the tail fixed on in the usual way. At (H) a short piece of trace wire (very fine) has been wound in with the silk and about 5mm has been left sticking straight up. A peacock harl has then been anchored with the silk to the body at (J). It has then been wound to the curve of the hook then back to within 2mm of the eye at (K).

A medium sized hackle about 60mm is then wound once round the hook and once round the upright wire of the pylon and repeated several times using the whole hackle to be locked in by the silk. The pylon tip is turned down firmly and held with silk to prevent the hackle from coming up and off. Pick out all the hackle fibre and "tease out" the peacock harl and you will have a true dry-fly which will "parachute" very gently down when cast out freely into the air.

When this fly is well oiled with floatant it will run along the surface of the water like thistle-down would behave, as it trundles with the breeze, and which I have seen being taken by a rising trout. At times I have had the sensation that the fly had to be pulled down on to the water as it reached the full distance of the cast. The finished fly should be treated in the same way as other dry-flies but it will be evident that it will not require the floatant renewed so often as the normal dry-fly.

When casting with the dry-fly on the river try to cast at an acute angle to the flow well above you, lift the rod at a rate to suit the strength of the current. Keep in touch and retrieve line by the overhand-wrist-twist method. Allow the fly to fish well down past you to the limit of the cast. By chance

Elements of Angling

if a fish is following allow the extended cast to come to your own side below and allow it to remain there for a few seconds before making the next cast, which should be a little further out so that, as the casts are made, a semi-elliptical area is covered. When satisfied that you have covered all parts which can be reached step 4 or 5 metres up stream and repeat the whole process to cover the next area. Approach the fish from behind and you have less chance of being seen. It is amazing how a dry-fly will ride on the surface of quite strict water. In most circumstances allow the fish time to go down again before striking. I try to count three before I make a move and strike firmly.

There are many floatants on the market; oils, pastes and greases and spray types and all have their particular advantages. I prefer to take a well soaked piece of felt and rub the line and cast while it is folded into two and hold the fly gentle in it. Should it be necessary to change casts ample oil is put on the felt, and part of the line is done over again, but change of flies means dipping them into my special solution.

Preparation of Floatant

Warm as much turpentine or substitute as would fill an egg-cup and dissolve in it a piece of candle wax (paraffin wax) about the size of a butter bean. Do not heat very much only sufficiently to melt the wax. Allow it to cool slowly. Some of the wax will re-form, but most of it will stay in the solution in the turpentine. If overheated there is the risk of fire. Before attempting to make use of the floatant be sure it is cold enough to work. Put it into a small medicine bottle with a spent match bruised at the end, to act as a brush, stuck firmly in the cork stopper.

When a fly has been coated, waft it through the air for about 10 seconds to dry it, then drop it in the water to allow the extra turpentine to float away before it is presented to the fish, which otherwise might sense the oil and be scared off.

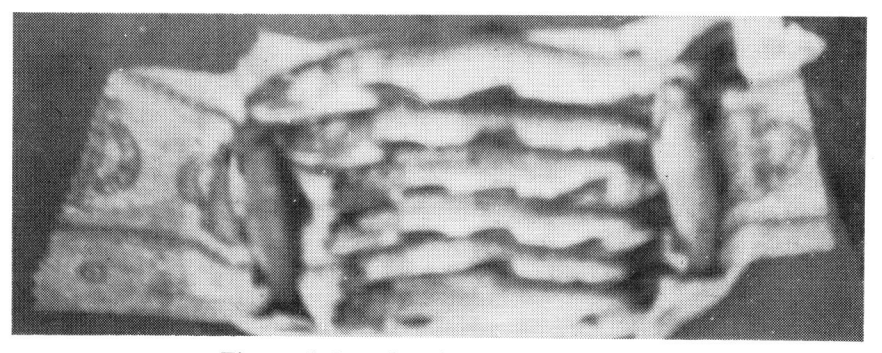

Figure 5. 2 A Good Evening's Fishing

Records of Catches

From my records I quote the following:

"12th June 1956 and at Pow's Dam. 7pm to 9.45pm 8 trout on a cast of three flies, Greenwell Glory, Grey Spider and Bronze Coachman. Wind – warm south-westerly light breeze, bright sun at times, with mostly a cover with white cloud. The air was warmer than the water.

1 Trout at 1 $^3/_4$ lbs, 1 at 1 lb, 2 at 12 ozs, 2 at 8 ozs, and 2 at 7 ozs and 7 others were returned to the water, which were of taking size and five smaller ones also returned"

Dapping

Fishing using the wind and having a very fine floss line is termed as Dapping. With the lightest floss line used there need only be a zephyr disturbing the quiet air to attempt dapping. The word itself practically signifies the method, because with a gentle air-flow, the line will rise and dip until it gently lands on the surface of the water. On a day when the wind is just a little stronger, a great distance can be attained while dapping, but should the movement of the air be moderate or more, difficulty will be experienced in causing the fly to settle on the water. In truth, with the lightest floss or making use of a cast of around 2 lbs. B.S. the line can whip in the wind and "Crack off the fly".

The fly to use should be small – say about No. 14 hook similar to that used when fishing with a horse-hair cast, and should be of the gnat or spider type and dressed as a dry-fly. It is seldom necessary to use any floatant on the fly, nevertheless I have used the candle-wax – turpentine preparation with less wax in it than for normal dry-fly fishing. Flies with light bands of narrow tinsel are preferred, to save weight and should be used in good light, for reflection of the light seems to be more attractive to trout in quiet waters, especially if the air is warmer than the water.

There are instances where it is very tantalising to see trout rise so far out that normal casting with the fly cannot reach them. If even a quiet wind is blowing this method of dapping can be used. It can also be employed to advantage in places round the shore of a loch, or on the banks of larger rivers under high banks or where trees, shrubs or other waterside growths make it difficult for normal casting. Set up the dapping tackle and although much experience and not a little skill are called for, some of these awkward places hold an extra fish or two, waiting to reward extra effort put into preparing the tackle for dapping.

When a fish does rise while dapping, do not strike; allow the fish ample time before lifting the rod gently to take up the strain. The rod used for dapping should be very light and yieldy so that the strain can be absorbed by it to be easy on the line. Be prepared to spend much more time before attempting to bring the fish to the net. One memorable success while dapping was on Loch Invar, near Dalry, Galloway when I took a fish of 1 lb. 5oz. the second largest trout of the day's competition. A fair breeze was blowing constantly from the top of the loch and by choosing the places on the shore on the lea side of the small bays I managed to take three others all under the 3/4 lb., but was not placed in the competition to which I had been invited as a guest. It was a clear day and on occasion a trout could be seen as it approached the fly in the quieter ripples. I had to discipline myself to wait on the fish hooking itself. This is very difficult to do if you have been casting with a normal cast of flies previously.

Should the breeze fade to a near-calm, the best method, to keep up a degree of expectancy, is to cast on leisurely and immediately a fish rises within casting distance attempt to cast into the rings before the trout has gone far down. I resorted to this method on Paisley Reservoir; Camphill Dam, one sunny June day and took 8 reasonable trout and put 10 small ones back. My two companions fishing in the same way took 9 and 5 trout of taking size, respectively. I have tried casting into the rings made by fish with a normal cast of wet flies also of dry flies but never can I say that the results were as thrilling as they were on that particular occasion.

Conditions for fishing

Frequently we hear "Fish won't be taking today" or "They won't rise in this kind of weather – It is too cold". "It's too bright" Sometimes "ower early", sometimes "ower late", sometimes "nae watter". It may also be "a spate", as is stated in the lines of the "Angler's Lament". All sorts of excuses are given if the angler returns home with an empty creel. Then there are all the hard-luck stories, which we have heard form time to time, all too frequently told as face-savers to gain the sympathy of the listener. But don't be sceptical of the empty creel for there are a few who go to the water to prove that some established rule on the conditions for fishing may be suspect. Many a time and oft when the "fit" was on me, I have set out to do just that.

Especially have I tried to prove or disprove that there are always exceptions to the rule. *On occasion I have landed a salmon on a day when a hot sun was beating overhead. I have landed trout during a thunder storm.*

Elements of Angling

This I would not recommend to anyone. No one knows where lightning will strike. Nevertheless, there are recognised rules to be obeyed and some to be respected when considering conditions for and against going out to fish. There is also the element of luck which plays a part in almost all sports.

If some of us cannot always be patient enough to wait for the correct conditions, then why not have a go occasionally. It must surely be from the efforts of such experimenting anglers, which established many of the unwritten rules in the first place. No matter how rigidly our conceptions of the established rules regarding fishing conditions become fixed in our minds, there is always the hope that our own success may be the exception. If such incidents are repeated often enough a new rule could be established.

We have already dealt with conditions as they apply to fishing the bait, early and during a spate, let us look at some other aspects, where the conditions are considered to be important. We have seen how the bait would be used at the beginning of a spate and as the spate continues to rise to a full water and the fishing position of the bait alters and as the heavy spate still continues and you have given up, to return after the rains have ceased and as the dirty brown water gradually goes down and changes to the colour of dark wine and then to a clearer wine colour, it is usually found that the bait becomes less attractive to any kind of fish.

We must therefore change our tactics : At the first sign of the water clearing start spinning with a minnow or mepp. Any artificial lure will suit but keep the size large to commence with, 2" to 2 1/2" should take salmon, seatrout and large trout, but if for trout only 1 1/4" to 1 3/4" might do. As the water clears, lures should become smaller – for trout as small as 3/4" and down to 1 1/2" for salmon. At a stage which will be determined from experience and usually when the light colour of wine is reached, a cast of large flies may given the answer desired. Flies on hooks of not less than size No. 8. This is the best time for stout tube-flies and flies of the long type on tandem hooks. As the water sinks to its lowest level you may find success with much smaller types. I once hooked a monster fish with a seatrout cast of No. 12 hooks and this fish was attached for one hour and five minutes before the small hook wore out. A friend who was at my side during the most of that time estimated that that salmon must have been on the 45 lb mark. One of my hard luck stories which was unsuccessful because of the size of the fish.

Regarding the conditions at the end of a spate, often there is a period when the methods of fishing seem to overlap; a period when flies and spun lures may both be accepted by fish still wandering about in search of suitable "lies". One such case comes to mind. An invitation came to myself and friend Harry and we set out in the early evening to sample the fishing on Kilmore stretch of the Doon and we found the conditions very similar to these stated.

Elements of Angling

The water was down to normal level after a spate but still had a slight wine coloured tinge. We commenced by fishing minnow and spoon alternately and when nothing happened, after some time, I thought I would try the fly. No sooner had I started to cast to a likely lie when an obliging salmon attached itself to my cast and refused to be shaken off. So between us we landed a nice cock fish just over 9 lbs. Naturally both of us fished fly for a considerable time afterwards without incident of any kind and as the light began to fail I thought on the idea of the overlapping time for the different lures so we both changed back to the minnow lure and my friend landed a fish of similar proportions to my one within 10 minutes of changing. His lure was a 1 1/2" devon and not long after, I took a fish about 2 lbs. less on a flat home made type of the same size. It would seem that during conditions like these the fish should be given a choice for after all it is sometimes the fish's last choice?

Figure 5.3 Preparing for the Evening Rise

The Evening Rise

Some very pleasant memories of fishing the evening rise will linger long with me. Would that they could be repeated but alas more and more fishers are taking part in the sport today, even where I fish, to allow that to happen. The evening rise should not be missed in the correct conditions nor should the twilight half-hour; the witching-hour we call it in our part of the country. It is preferred to take these two times as distinct fishing times as there are some subtle differences between them.

If the cold easterly winds are blowing early in the evening you may as well sit by the fire for all that will happen. Few fish of any kind move during an east wind and although the wind may be of assistance in casting because of the lie of the river, do not be tempted.

However be it warm; the air warmer than the water and the wind in almost any other quarter of the compass you should venture forth. Start fishing about 7 pm of any day between mid May and late August when the heat of the day lingers long enough to keep the flies yoyoing over the sedges and with a cast of three smallish flies on a finely tapered cast visit a number of undisturbed pools in turn and if fish are there, you can have a very pleasurable evening. See photo on page 79 for results of just hitting the correct conditions and time.

Fishing at Dusk

Settle down at the head or bottom of a pool every detail of which you are fondly familiar. Prepare your tackle as if you expect nothing but seatrout of the strong variety. Therefore have tackle stronger than for trout. The cast should be made up with two flies only and need not be larger than No. 12.

Select them from the following: *Black Spider, Grey Spider* with silver body, *Silver Butcher*, *Teal and Blue*, *Teal and Green*, *Woodcock* and *Yellow* with yellow gantron or any other similar fly.

The fly is usually taken very gently, therefore it is suggested to delay striking for about three seconds after the fish is felt. You will seldom see them until they actually commence to fight.

As was suggested in up-stream worming the fish should be played within the confines of an area which will not seriously disturb the part being fished. If this can be done easily a return to casting can commence almost immediately the fish is netted.

Elements of Angling

Night Fishing

We usually associate seatrout only when we mention night fishing but I have been fortunate to take large trout and salmon during the hours of darkness. This type of fishing, given that conditions are the same, is very much the same as for fishing at dusk, however, there are a few important differences. Chief among these is the question of wading. Be sure that you know every inch of any area which is to be waded and it is also advisable to note any awkward parts of the bank. It is therefore advised that careful study of the area both in the water and around it before attempting to fish in the dark when distances are more difficult to estimate. I can testify to that by an incident that happened to me. My cast became snagged on a branch sticking out of the water and to save it I ventured two steps further out and failed to touch the bottom and get a sound soaking. Discretion is the better part of valour on such occasions?

SO TAKE THE HINT? GET TO KNOW EVERY STEP OF THE WAY , **before you think of entering the water.**

It is generally found that a light coloured fly of almost any dressing will suit for night fishing, but my best results have been achieved with thickly dressed flies of darker colours with a glinting body. But for most of my results I have been well served with almost any fly as long as two or three fly –maggots were attached to it. It seems to me that the movement of the grubs on the hook is a greater attraction to seatrout than any form of dressing that can be invented. One thing which must be carefully considered in night fishing is to maintain silence. Talk only if necessary and this should be in whispers , for if noises should exceed the sounds of the streamy waters, seatrout will remain subdued.

Figure 5.4 Casting into the Rings at Dawn

Another good time to fish is just as the dawn is breaking. When you hear the little robin red breast leading the dawn chorus, get out your gear and prepare a cast of averaged sized flies. Something which glints the subtle morning lights, the *Silver Butcher, Greenwell's Glory* or some of the teals. Cast, in the beginning, in the streams above the pools and gradually move down into the pools, hopefully following interested fish. Keep fishing for the hour after dawn right down into the chosen pool. Some anglers aware that

Elements of Angling

the best times are at the hours around noon others that the time of day even on inland water coincides with the hour before and the hour or so after high tide. But I have long come to the conclusion that anglers fishing during the times which have previously been successful for them will satisfy them most.

THEORIES ON FISHING TIMES

Many anglers, who fish in the sea from rocky or deep shores, prefer to commence casting about one hour before high tide and may wish to continue for about the same time thereafter. There are also numbers of inland anglers, who, noting that these sea-anglers assume that the presence of feeding fish near the deeper shores is most evident during these hours, are sometimes conscious that the fish of the river and land-locked water follow a similar pattern. They believe rightly or wrongly that this is a lingering legacy from the habits of fish many million years ago, when oceans covered almost all of the earth's surface and when all fish were free to roam all over the globe and were therefore in a position to be influenced by the tides. The duration of the high tide seems to be the main feeding times for many sea creatures and since the tides are caused by the gravitational pull of both Sun and Moon there has been from time to time great interest in this speculation. This fishy phenomenon became known as the "Solar-Lunar Theory", which has been abbreviated to "Solunar Theory".

Several years ago this theory was faithfully followed by many of the keenest anglers; especially the "FLY-Purists", but now it seems to command very little attention, if any. Even the present-day periodicals seldom refer to it. Now it is being restudied. If there is any basis for its application, can it be one of these intriguing mysteries of nature, such as the migration of birds, beasts, fish or what have you. Does it compare with the mysterious "homing" of the blue-bar pigeons from places hundreds of miles away or the suicidal impulses of the teeming lemmings as they hurl themselves into the sea, to balance out their numbers – or is it just another unsolved peculiarity that remains from the far and distant past that has puzzled the students of evolution down the ages. Perhaps science, which has come up with some acceptable reasons for many other phenomena may put forward some explanation for the suspected Solunar Theory on the peak feeding times of fish to satisfy the enquiring mind of the sophisticated angler.

Although that issue may still be in doubt; meantime the theoretical angler may wish to give this theory some consideration and at the same time also give ear to other theories manifest by many others as yielding some tangible results. There is the theory that "Dawn and Dusk" are the best times to fish, especially with fly; wet or dry, depending on the whim of the angler. On further consideration it is perfectly obvious that there will be few evenings or dawns together, when the "Dawn to Dusk" conception will coincide with the Solunar Theory. This will occur twice for each lunar month. This factor should be noted while making comparisons. The writer tried to prove the connection between the two about a quarter a century ago, but he found, that it is true to say, that so many other factors had to be allowed for, that no definite conclusion was reached. There are for example – temperature changes, changes in the intensity of light, changes in wind force and direction and others. All play their part to some degree in affecting the rising fish. Nevertheless having made a true study of the high tides time table and taking accurate notes other anglers may produce enough evidence to acclaim or condemn this Solnar Theory. It is also possible that some new factors could be discovered to influence the behaviour of hungry fish.

Some anglers I have met, who swear by the "Noon–rise", the "Mid Afternoon Rise" or the "Early Evening Rise" may never have studied the Solunar Theory, or if they have known of it have not taken it to heart could have, by chance, hit on the true feeding time around the peak of the tide but unknown to them.

If many more anglers were to keep an eye on the tide charts, that are published in most local papers and make comparison with the times of rising or taking fish perhaps more conclusive evidence would be forthcoming. There are many; very many, who neglect all theories and fish only when heavy spates are running and often with a great amount of success. Although spate conditions would seem to be exempt from such theories, still notes kept during spates also might reveal some surprising conclusions.

Another theory that a close friend of mine liked to elaborate on comes from the following:

> *If nature is merry in voice today*
> *And Birds all bursting with song*
> *You will find the fishes are ready to play*
> *And the urge to feed comes along.*

This verse sums up his theory very well. In truth this friend grew to believe so strongly in his theory, that he practiced imitating many of the songs of the riverside warblers and actually relied upon his own whistled tunes to spread a feeling of joy amid the companions of his own "solitude" in his attempts to tempt the timid trout to try his tackle. On the other hand he believed as follows :

> Too bright the day that tempts the dragon–fly,
> On vibrant wing yo–yoing to the sky

Elements of Angling

Pack-up your casts and line and trundle home
With Sun thus bright be sure no fish will roam

The evening rise just before and after sunset seems to serve most anglers best of all, but some anglers spend more time on the water then, than at any other time. This is much the same assessment of successes conjured by the anglers, who prefer a certain type of fly and therefore cast with little else and automatically conclude: that, that particular fly is the best, yet it could have happened that a fly of some other choice might have served him better. I myself have my own preferences, but not to the exclusion of all others. I believe as in many other spheres of activity – variety is the spice of life, yet to carefully compare notes, while following any theoretical whim can be very interesting, illuminating and perhaps in the long-run rewarding.

Waders and Wading

Although it has been stated that the beginner may be advised at the outset to obtain a tall pair of wellington boots for wading purposes, there comes a time when he will become dissatisfied with the limits which are thus imposed on him. If he is angling on larger waters and wider streams and at places difficult to reach, he will soon feel at a disadvantage or if he observes some experienced angler find success in some distant "lies" then the urge to purchase longer foot-gear will be stepped up.

Angler's waders can be got in two main types:

1. Thigh-waders, which usually reach up to the crutch of the leg on the inside and a bit longer on the outside, and have straps which are attached to the trouser-braces by two adjustable loops;

2. Full-waders, which come right up to the chest, and are most usually made of rubberised canvas, have straps over the shoulders, but are encased over the feet, by a pair of stout heavily studded boots or deep shoes.

The latter, I would not recommend to any one who has not had some experience with the former. It may not seem obvious to the inexperienced person, but there is a special technique to be mastered in the use of full-waders. Because of the tendency of the feet to lift upwards and float, if the angle at which the leg is held is too great. These waders should be gradually mastered in still water or in streams that are not very deep. The safe angle of the leg must be carefully judged and therfore I would recommend that the shorter thigh-length waders should be the natural follow on from the wellington boots. The thigh-length waders can be of the studded type or have

Elements of Angling

deeply grooved all rubber designed soles. Get to know the nature of the bed of the waters being fished. All rubber soles can slip badly on weedy banks and glutty river beds especially if the bed is all rocky or covered in large boulders. Wading on gravel, sand or shingle beds will, in nearly all cases, be safer, but if it is thought that raw sewage or partially treated related materials are present, make sure that you obtain waders with good strong studs.

Water levels

Some proprietors and clubs are very particular regarding which methods of fishing can be employed during different levels of river water. Some have installed a water-level-gauge at a strong position on the bank as a guide. Fishing with the bait may only be permitted during a spate and must cease when the water goes down to a certain level and when the level is a certain amount below that again, only the fly will be allowed. A few clubs have similar rules but are more lax in applying such restrictions than the private owners. At maximum levels most rivers cannot be fished by any means because the would-be angler would be fishing on top of the grass.

As already mentioned in the lesson on waders sudden changes in the level of the water, such as those caused by rains from a cloud-burst can be hazardous. I remember fishing a private stretch near home, when, in less than half-an-hour, cloud-burst water swelled the river, which was earlier showing its "bare bones" right up to its maximum. We, my father-in-law and myself sensed what was about to take place and took precautions, but later we learned that several got into difficulties further down stream.

6

PIKE AND PERCH

Alternative Fishing

Although the waters in the close proximity of my domicile are not given to fishing for Perch and Pike, I have gone further away from home and have gained some experience in this kind of angling and some of this experience is herewith passed on, so that the reader may indulge himself in this side of the sport. During what is termed the closed season for game fish; trout, seatrout and salmon, a growing number of anglers, find an outlet for their strong desire to fish all the year round, by fishing for Perch and Pike. Others find some consolation in angling for the winter sporting fish; the Grayling.

On occasion I have, along with a keen angling friend, broken the ice on the surface of a loch (only when the ice was thin) in order to spin an artificial minnow, plug or spoon in the shallow edges or in waters near the reeds.

Safety precautions are definitely the first consideration when fishing for the fierce pike. It is advisable to attach the lure to the line with a length of elasticum trace wire instead of the usually cast of nylon, because the teeth of the Pike are so arranged that they can cut through that material easily. To protect the hands while unhooking a pike with its sharp sloping teeth, it is advised to have at hand short pieces of stout wood to keep the mouth of the fish open.

As to perch care should be taken to avoid the strong spikes or spines on the dorsal fin and do not expect a perch to have completely succumbed although it may have been in the creel for a half-a-day. Perch have been known to be still alive by late evening after being taken from the water at noon.

Where it is suspected that very large pike are lurking and you hope to attract them, your fixed spool reel should have ample nylon of not less than 12 B.S. and have that metre of heavy trace wire, already mentioned, attached by means of two or three half-hitches and the end of the wire turned round itself several times. With the changing of lures the end of the wire may break off and gradually the wire becomes shorter and shorter. Therefore always carry extra wire with you at all times.

Hungry pike are usually located in or near a partially decayed reed bed or between large stones in the shallows, but in deeper water he may lie under rock ledges and in darkened corners waiting for the unsuspecting trout or minnow. Therefore to know the formation of the stream or loch can be very helpful. As stated already – the best time to fish for pike is on a bright day after several dull ones. Try to get to the water as soon after the change in the weather takes place. The time of day does not matter so much. The type of lure to use in such circumstances can vary considerably: A small spoon or plug which need not be more than 2" to begin with, should be considered as ample. But as time goes on the size should be increased and after fishing the shallows try your largest lures to greater depths. Lastly it is usually necessary to fish with tempting baits – a large bunch of worms a good sized sprat or even half of a herring.

It is interesting to note that Pike and Perch can manage an existence together in the same water. This is perhaps because the perch is so well protected from the large toothy jaws of the pike of ferocious fame, by the strong spines making up part of the dorsal fin. The perch, because of its small mouth, can do little damage to the pike except when it comes across some pike spawn. They may go for very small pike in the shallows. Otherwise they live their lives "together" yet very much "apart". The pike in the darker shadows or in the deepest recesses and usually alone if large; the perch gathered together nearer the surface in shoals. We assume that nature has planned it that way for their protection. The smaller ones gathered in grater numbers. The numbers becoming less and less with the passage of time, due to depletion by the actions of man and other preyful creatures and by voluntary and involuntary segregation. The voluntary segregation may come about from the natural instincts – as they grow they will each require more food and will divide into smaller groups (shoals) so that the food to hand will be sufficient to go round. The availability of food will determine the size of the shoals. Involuntary segregation can come about from a sudden scare which will scatter them and they find difficulty in coming together again. Now there will be more than one shoal of smaller numbers.

The question has been asked: Do we get pike and perch in any of our rivers? Yes! of course we do and in quite a number of them. Would it be correct to say that they were not always there? This is difficult to answer, but it is generally believed that at one time they were indigenous to loch and lakes and were introduced to many rivers by the Monks who dwelt near the rivers in monasteries, for an easy supply of winter food. Odd rivers have to pass

Elements of Angling

The Pike
A fierce opponent which must be watched

The Perch

Figure 6.1 Illustrations of Pike & Perch

through lakes or lochs in which pike and perch thrive, therefore on occasion pike are found in the rivers themselves. I recall taking a **Pike-Perch enthusiast** to a slow part of just such a river hoping to show him how to cast for a reasonable sized trout. I went to the base of a burn which drains a loch about 2 miles long, where there are both pike and perch and after a few casts I landed a stout perch of 1 1/2 lbs. My friend from his previous experience was able to unhook it without touching the dreaded back fin. Next cast I hooked another but it got off and casting on another one followed by another. All of similar size were taken in about half an hour and although I continued for about another hour nothing more happened. This to me, helps to uphold the idea that this type of fish do move about in shoals.

It should again be stressed that the perch is more active on a bright spell after several days of dull or wet weather, but it can be so, also on a warm sultry summer's evening at about the mid evening. During the colder weather the bait proves more attractive and for the largest perch surface plugs of almost any form are acceptable. The last should be smaller than for pike, although there are times when both will go for the same type and size of this kind of lure. Usually expect the pike to take in the shadows or near long reeds and bullrushes, while the perch can be expected almost anywhere near the surface or close to gravelly shores.

Not that I would wish my young angler to follow the methods employed when I had my baptism to the ways of "angling" for pike and perch. It was "crude", very crude indeed and it is given to show that even in the crudest of methods there is much to be gained from the experience. In retrospect the tender age of 9 years is not too early to seek adventure and in searching for it my school chums and I had not far to look. We went fishing and while admitting that this was the cheapest method to do this form of fishing, it was great fun. Hooks and sinkers and a sturdy line with a short piece of trace wire were all fixed together. No rod! no reel! The fish when hooked was fought by hand, thus many which were lightly hooked got away. In those early days, the boys intent in using up the spare time were often to be found in the open spaces around the village and since there were three small lochs in the vicinity all carrying pike and perch, lots of the time was spent on their shores.

Using the above tackle plus a lemonade bottle as a float and the necessary bait, we proceeded thus:

> A short piece of thick cord was tied round the neck of the corked bottle and the line was passed through this cord so that it could be adjusted to have the bait at differing depths. The cast and hooks were attached and the bait was put on, then with a round-the-head swing, holding the line, the bottle, bait and all were projected well "into the middle mere" while the line, which lay beside the "fisher" would uncoil to follow in the wake

Elements of Angling

of the roughly directed tackle. The lot would hit the water with a terrible resounding splash, which must have scared the fish for some hundred yards. However, for all this disturbance, on the passing of a considerable time, sure enough there was movement on that floating bottle and there was a quick grab and strike on the line by the "fisher" and as often as not he was fighting a fish. Most of the bigger ones regained their freedom but many good pike and perch were taken in this way. Often there was more than one lying on the shore at the same time. Line fishing, we were to learn later was against the Law. It was not a case of "Where Angels Fear to Tread" but rather "Where Ignorance is Bliss". As experience was gained, we learned to have a short line below the bottle-float if we hoped to take perch, if for pike we had to judge that the line would be on or near the bottom. On the hooking of a big fish of over two pounds all would gather round (for there were usually half a dozen of us) to admire the catch and to discover as much as possible about the size of the bait, the depth of the line and where the fish was hooked. When a pike of enormous size was hooked the other lines were soon forgotten while the fun of trying to land the big one was observed and where required, help given.

Thus was experience gained, which was to be put to good use years later when the right kind of tackle and full gear were obtainable and when more spectacular fish were taken. It was a warm sultry evening on Loch Ken famous for its size of midges. Perhaps they are not as large as those to be encountered around Inch Mirron on Loch Lomond but they were as persistent.

When we managed to hold them partially at bay by repeated applications of repellant, an attempt was made to tempt the trout with fly from the shore. Almost at the first cast my companion rose and gravelled a trout of over one and a half pounds. I waited until he invited me and I cast into exactly the same spot where the trout had risen and there came to me a fish of the same type and size, or so I thought, but it turned out to be a long slim fish – a pike of about the same weight.

This is the only pike which I have taken on the fly, yet I have learned of others who have had such an experience.

It took a black spinner; a fly with black hackle, no wing and a silver body. It is well known that the pike are not popular for the table in this country, but I have been told by anglers from the continent that we here do not know the value of both perch and pike as we should?

Both as fighting fish and as delicacies for the table they have a lot to recommend them. I personally have enjoyed a fillet of perch, but I may have yet to learn how to cook pike to be satisfied with it.

Records

Before a beginner takes part in any serious angling he or she should give consideration to keeping a record of all outings. Fully detailed notes of all visits to the water, can be a great benefit for future reference. Dates and times of day; complete weather conditions with regard to cloud or shine, wind and temperature are worth recording along with the names and sizes of flies employed; also the types and sizes of spinning lures can add to the interest of the notes. These details in addition to the weights and sizes of all fish caught including any which had to be returned to the water.

Special notes on the success or failure of a fishing companion are sometimes worth noting, such as unfortunate incidents while playing a fish or at the landing can serve to prevent a similar occurrence in time to come.

The notes referring to "catch" can be very satisfying to the recorder but in addition some clubs and land-owners expect returns of all catches to be submitted, usually at the end of each season and these are preferred to be recorded month by month. A few anglers are reluctant to give these returns but this is really against their own interest as true returns can give a guide to the responsible parties estimating when restocking should be carried out and as to what extent.

Yes! record-keeping is a very serious but interesting part of the ardent angler's sport and can become a most valuable reference in many ways.

PART 4
MISCELLANEOUS TOPICS

From an old Print

7
MATERIALS FOR MAKING RODS

D.I.Y. or Purchasing?

At this point instruction could be given on the making of rods, for example the split-cane rod, but today fibre-glass and carbon rods are a more popular choice – almost to the exclusion of the split-cane type, which required time, patience and expert skills to complete, but which served the angling fraternity faithfully for generations.

During the latter years of that period, rod making firms produced kits of parts which could be made up by the more practical anglers themselves. Some of these included greenheart, lancewood or other suitable timber, while others had prepared rod sections of split tonkin cane or of slender-tapered, completely shaped stems of cane. All kits had a complete set of rings, cork-grips, reel fittings, silk, glue and varnish, with a sheet of instructions on how to complete the work. Most of the rods obtained in this way served the angler well, but some proved to be lacking in the finer points of balance and ability to cast well.

Now the manufacturers of rods kits and tackle are more conscious of the requirements of their customers and by the application of the more modern materials at their disposal, are producing more efficient, more reliable and much lighter rods to the delight of the most critical angler.

However, with all these advantages the choice of reel and line to suit the rods on the market is left to the angler himself and therefore the *balance* of the rod is now to be considered.

THE 'BALANCE' OF THE ROD

The **balance** of the rod is very important to all anglers, but some are more conscious of this than others. A rod very badly out of balance can be a tiring concern to anyone who likes his fishing in long spells at a time. A rod, which is top heavy especially, can become very straining on the muscles of wrists and arms and if it is a fairly large rod the back muscles can become affected also. Since it does take time to accentuate this constant straining

Elements of Angling

against the weight of the rod, which has its centre of gravity at a point well up from the butt, one would think that most anglers would sense this fault at the first handling. It takes a bit of experience to do this. Many can say that there is something wrong with rod in question, but few can tell the exact fault. However, if technical knowledge on the "balance of the rod" does anything, it should show that with a little bit of study, the keen angler will find out faults for himself. We sometimes hear the comment "it's no use, it sends out the line all squiggly" and the rod itself is blamed for this, when all that is wrong, is that the reel and line are too heavy for the rod. How do we know this? Some will say "by experience in handling." Yes! that is possible, but there is a way to tell the behavioural characteristics of a rod before an attempt is made to cast with it and this can be forecast in the following way:

Study sketches in **Figure 7.1** and note the directions of arrows (A), (C) and (B). (A) is that point where the weight of the reel plus the weight of the line in the reel act through and (B) is where the weight of the rod itself acts through, while (C) is where they both act through, i.e. the C.G. centre of gravity.

In the case of the trout rod of orthodox proportions it will be held in one of two positions in one hand while the other hand is free to manipulate the line. Now comes the personal touch which distinguishes one angler from another, when each gives a contradictory opinion on the same rod.

Note at figure (C) the C.G. is in front of the fore finger and that the rod is not pressed down by the thumb, though the thumb might be just touching it; while at (D) the C.G. is in the hand and is behind the fore-finger. This necessitates pressure from the thumb to keep the tip of the rod in position. Whether you are conscious of this fact or not, the C.G. of an apparently balanced rod, with reel and line having an amount of line drawn off to represent the amount being used while casting, will be somewhere between these two points. We shall have the two extremes of opinion as where the C.G. should be. Whether I am right or wrong in my choice matters little, but I prefer the first position given. I have reasoned it this way:

> When a fish is felt nerves have to obtain a reaction from one set of muscles to strike, while if the other way, pressure must be taken off before the instant strike? The time saved is infinitesimal, but the reaction of some trout is faster than our own. So every little time saved is crucial. But to counter this idea, you could refer to the Push Strike on sketch (Fig. 3.12), where of course the argument would mean that you hold your rod in the other manner. The aim in all this is to have a rod so balanced and held in such a way that you will not tire yourself out during a full day's fishing. You will also be all the more alert to strike at a taking fish. A rod which is only a small amount out of balance

Elements of Angling

will not make all that amount of difference but one that is markedly out will not only tire but will distress the operator because of its inaccuracy and other peculiarities.

If you are sufficiently interested you can work out as suggested herewith, the position of the C.G. for any of your rods and especially if you were to attempt to construct a rod for yourself you would find this very helpful.

Weigh the rod by itself and let us say that is close to 5 ozs. weigh the reel and the line with about 6 to 8 metres of line lying on the floor. This allows for the amount of line run off while casting. Assume they weigh 13 ozs. which means that the reel and line weigh 8 ozs. Next balance the rod by itself on your fore finger and measure the distance from your finger to the butt end of the rod and carefully find the distance from the centre of the reel to the butt end also. In the rod I have to hand, these distances were 32" and 3" respectively. (see diagram) Let (x) be the distance from the butt end to where the C.G. will be located and equating we will get:

$$13X = (5 \times 32) + (8 \times 3)$$

$$\therefore 13X = 160 + 24 = 184/13 = 14.15"$$
from the butt of the rod

Should you wish to apply this work-out for a new rod the reel may be fixed by means of cellotape at different positions and with a little weight added to make up for the ferrules which hold on the reel in its permanent position. In this way the desired position of the C.G. can be fixed within the given limits. Adjustments can be made in several ways – more or less backing can be controlled in the reel, a heavier or lighter reel may be required; the position of the reel can be changed and if need be more cork rings can be added to the grip.

In the sketch (7.2) is shown the approximate position of the C.G. of a salmon rod, which is cast using both hands. The calculations for this rod are exactly the same as for a trout rod, but it will be realised that the rod being longer and of greater girth all the way the C.G. will be a greater distance from the butt end. See Fig. 7.2. This is shown at (A) and this means a long cork grip so that the rod is much more easily handled and the leading hand can quite easily reach the line to lock while casting or fighting a fish. If it is anticipated to continue casting for some time without resorting to change, it is recommended that the rod be held immediately after each cast as at (C) The second hand is transferred to behind the reel and the rod held closer to the body. This is a very restful position.

Elements of Angling

Note : I can remember an old angler, who could cast from this position, the arms extending very little. Look at the sketch on page 102, based on the author's practice and it will be seen that a cast is made with arms extended and immediately the cast has reached the entry point the arms will come back to the close position for the fishing out of the cast. This is a halfway stage which I have adopted towards the end of a full day's salmon fishing.

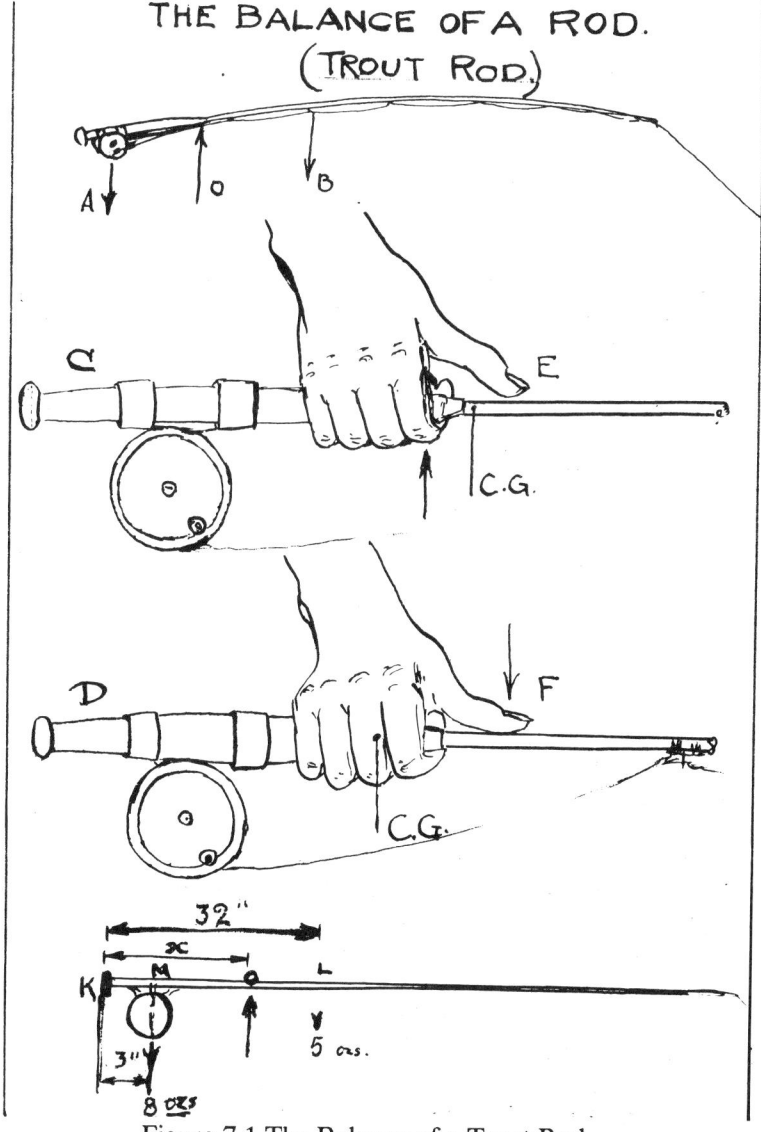

Figure 7.1 The Balance of a Trout Rod

Elements of Angling

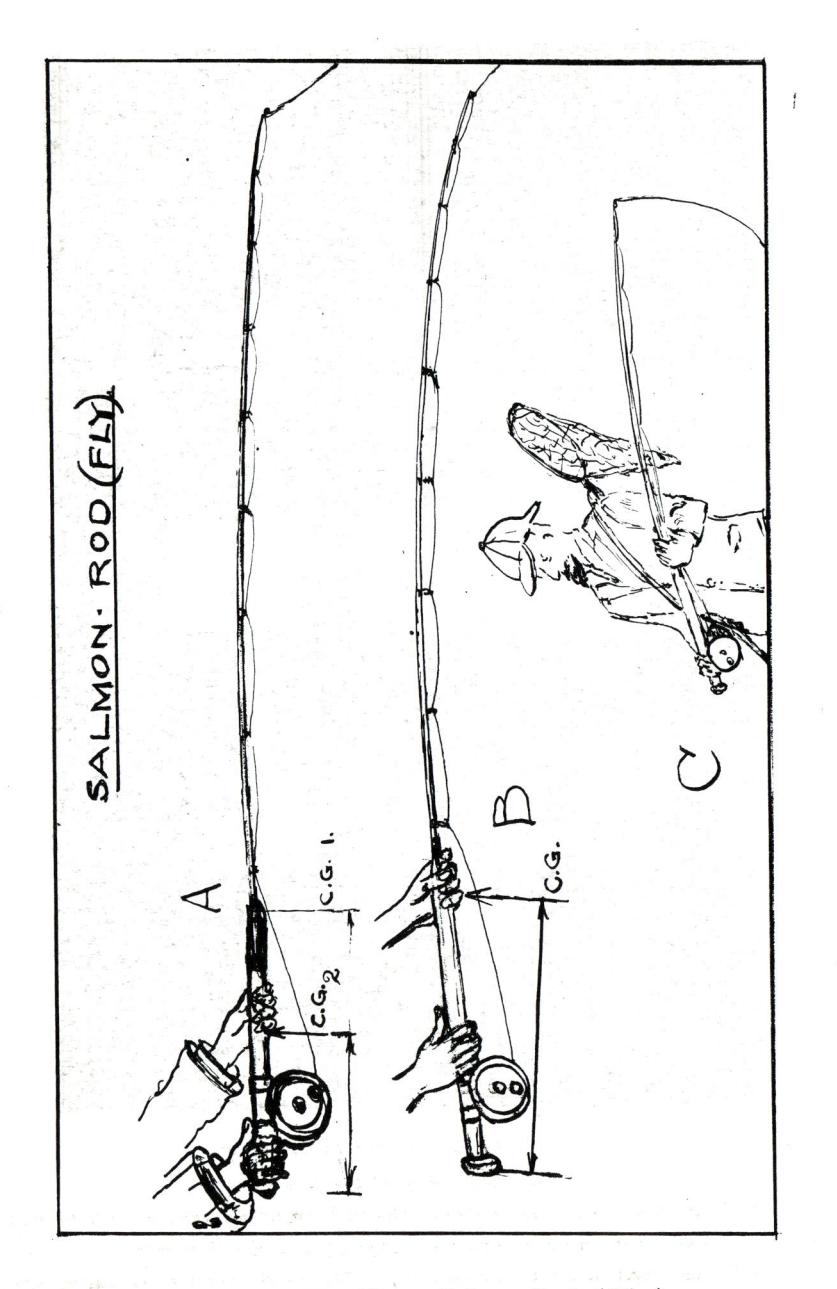

Figure 7.2 Handling a Salmon Rod (Fly)

Elements of Angling

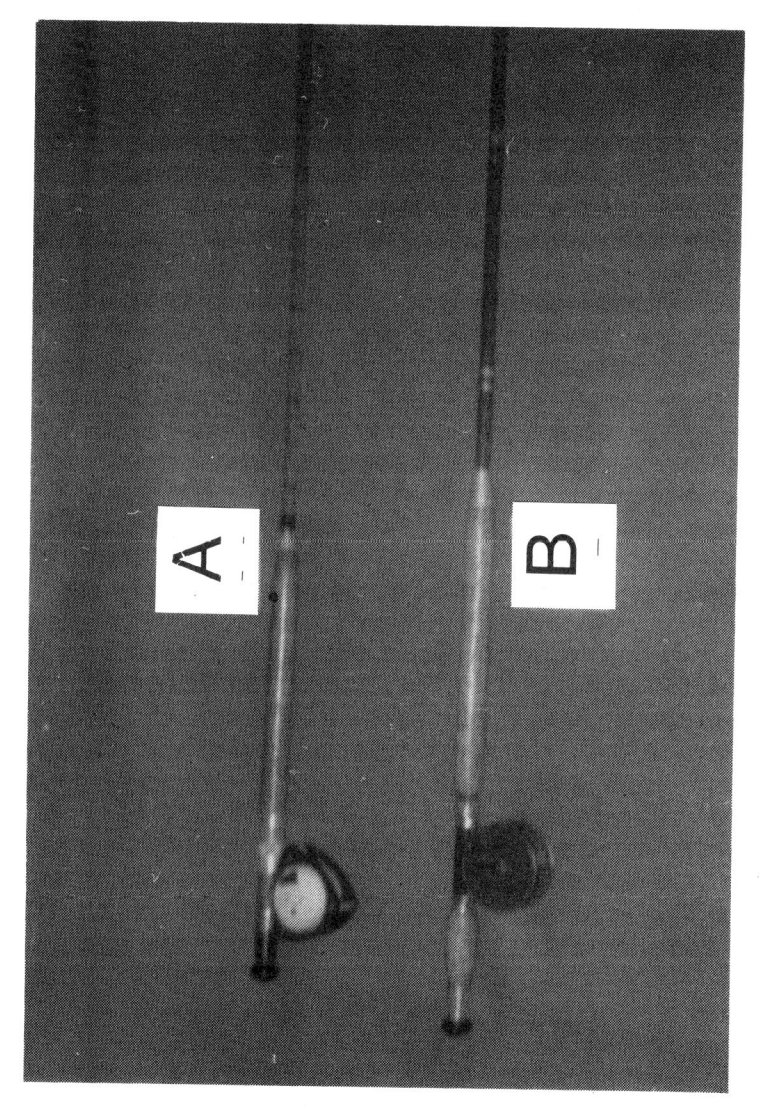

Figure 7.3 Further details on Balancing
The accompanying photograph shows:
at "A" the length of cork and position of the reel to maintain balance in a trout rod for single-hand casting of a 9ft. rod. A home produced split cane rod
at "B" the longer cork butt with the position of the heavier reel for two handed casting of a 12ft. salmon rod, A "Glass" rod made up from a "kit"

Elements of Angling

7.4 Fishing the Fly for Salmon on a clearing spate
The author with home made rod of split-cane 12' 6" type
Take note of two-hand grip

Fixing on the Rings

At Figure No. 7.5 are illustrated the different types of rod rings.
(F)   The simple snake ring is perhaps the most popular type.
(G)   The plain bridge ring efficient and keeps the line close to the rod.
(H)   Stand-off ring which keeps the line away from the rod but is susceptible to accidents because it is so far away from the rod.
(J)   Here is a ring found on many of the older rods. It is used for parking the tip hook while moving from pool to pool.

No matter the type they are all fixed to the rod in the same manner. If you are re-ringing an old rod or making a new one, determine the number of rings to be used and selecting them according to their sizes mark out their positions. Start at the butt. Form a perfectly large loop at (B) and commence to wind on the silk thread in such a way that the loop is trapped. Keep winding with the taut thread by holding the rod out in front at right angles to the thread and keep turning the rod towards you on the top as mentioned in repairing a rod. Cut the thread with ample to spare and pass (R) through the loop and pass under (S) draw tightly and trim off as at (D3) and (D4). Proceed to the second half in the same way. Note at (E) is the fixing of the tip-ring. This being a longer whipping means that it is more difficult to draw the thread through at the end. However, if an attempt is made to have the thread close to one of the legs or prongs of the ring for the loop, the finishing may be made easier.

Elements of Angling

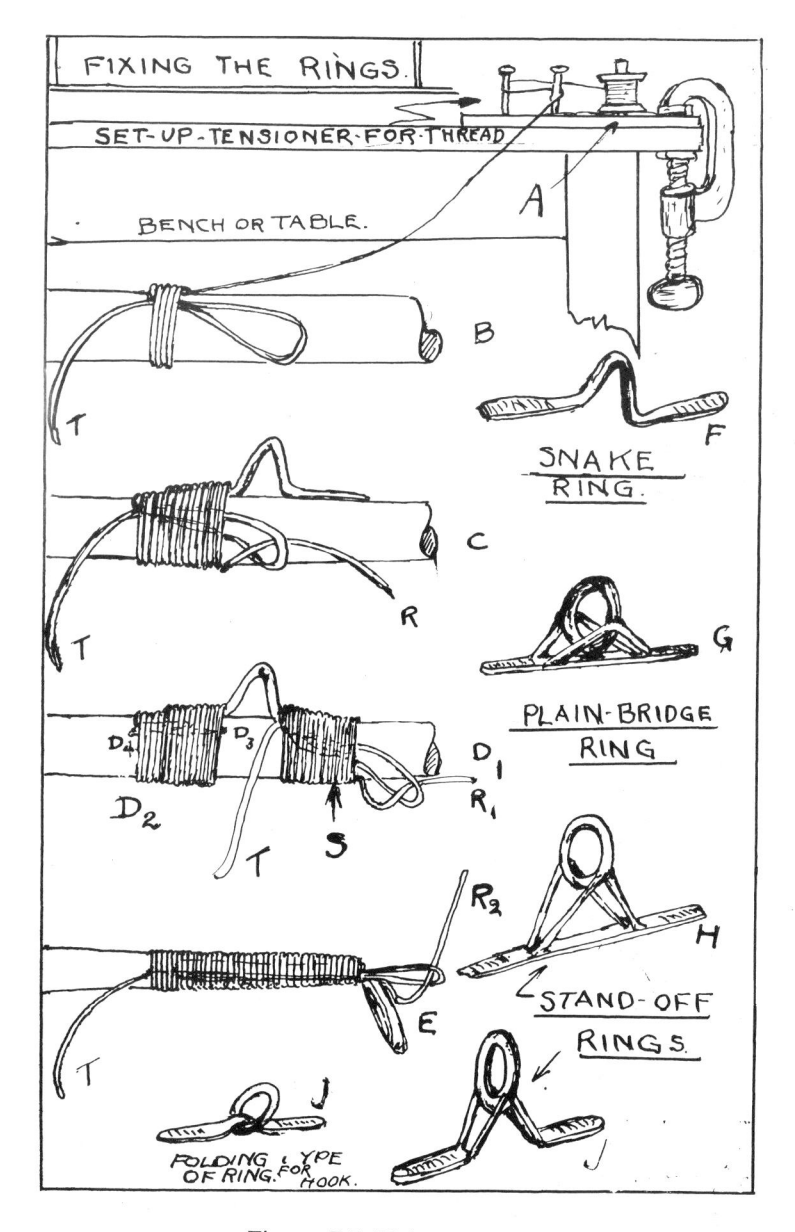

Figure 7.5 Fixing the Rings

Intermediate whipping or whipping of repairs is usually done in the same way. All whipping should receive a coat of spirit varnish or of celere.

Elements of Angling

I have used clear UHU glue, on occasion, for this purpose.

Rod Repairs

Most anglers prefer to have any rod repairs attended to by experts by sending them all carefully parcelled up to the manufacturers or by taking them to the tackle shop where is someone capable of doing the job, but the keen angler has on occasion to do small repairs for himself. An instance comes to mind – a club I was attached to organised an outing to Loch Spallander, at that time a natural loch but which since had been dammed up to give a water reserve for the central industrial estates. We arrived at a farm and had to walk the last half mile along a beaten track. On climbing over a stone wall a large boulder was removed and it landed on my rod, with the result that the tip for about 9" had to be removed. I was left with about two inches above the second top ring. It was a split cane rod so I took my pocket knife and removed the shattered part. I took off that second top ring and replaced it with the top ring. Although I felt a little awkward while casting at first and scared that my quick whipping on the ring might fail, I kept my fingers crossed and to everyone's surprise I managed to take 4 trout to secure 2nd place in the competition. Since then I have always carried a spool of thread for such an emergency. Once home again the repair may be completed in a more substantial manner.

See the diagrams on No. 7.5 for assistance in this.

The clamp holding the block of wood with the controlling nails can be fixed to a table or a bench. The thread is wound round the nail to put a suitable tension on it while whipping. The strength of the thread will turn the bobbin. Do not attempt to wind the thread round the rod part in any other method than described – rather sit a distance away from the table and keep turning the rod towards you on top while keeping the thread from forming spaces, yet not allowing it to ride on top of the last turns. When completed draw the end of the thread through the loop as shown and cover with a thin coat of spirit varnish.

Should you break a carbon rod here is a tip which might be applied.
Obtain a steel knitting pin which fits snugly into the hollow carbon. Glue about 2" inches into each part. Allow it to set. Cover the break for about an inch on each side of the break with fine adhesive tape then wind silk thread in the usual way. Give the whole repair a coat of varnish. I repaired one in this way some two years ago and it is still casting well.

Elements of Angling

Care of Equipment

The true successful angler becomes very attached to the equipment and tackle he has selected to suit his ways of fishing down the years and will guard against the possibility of anything happening to them, which might impair their efficiency. He will look upon each item as a fine piece of "bone china". Therefore at any sign of deterioration, he will have it attended to immediately and whether mishap or not at the end of each season he will look over all his equipment–rods, reels, lines, nets, tailers, and lures. Even his creel and/or fishing bag will not be omitted. Rods checked, repaired if necessary and given a thin coat of varnish. Seldom will rods made of fibre–glass or the very efficient carbon types require anything other than a good clean and placed in their covers.

The end of the season means attention to lines also. He will take all silk lines from their reels and put them on to line driers. Ample amounts of oil will be put into partially dismantled reels and vaseline will be smeared over any metal parts on the outside. Tailers and gaffs can be varnished on wooden parts and smeared with vaseline on metal parts. The net itself if more than three years old may be given a coat of linseed oil thinned down with turpentine, after being checked for weak strands.

He will not be at a loss as to how to store such lures as artificial minnows, plugs and spoons. He will retouch any colouring which has been chipped off; refurnish any bare metal parts and hone any hook points which have lost their keenness.

Storing Casts

A young angler may be at a loss as to how he should store made–up casts. Here are a few methods of tackling this chore.

After former experience with the usual Cast-Books, I have come to the conclusion that such books even with their thick felt "pages" are not all that can be desired in the way of keeping flies in their original state. The flies lose their fine fluffy appearance and soon become very flat. They are liable to fish differently in the water. They are apt to go through the water in a similar way to a mine–sweeping vane. Since this became evident to me, I began to look around for more suitable methods of storing fly casts. I tried old envelopes; A fly cast was put in each and they were placed one on top of the other in a cast box. This was a slight improvement. I tried separating them with a disc of thin cardboard the size of the inside of the cast box, but if more than one cast was placed in the box still some pressure was put on the flies.

These were my methods for many years until ultimately I have gone

Elements of Angling

further and gained much more satisfaction. There are plastic discs on the market, which are so constructed at the edges to allow the cast to be coiled out and in the projecting parts. There are usually eight of these parts. Using the same principle I cut thin cardboard discs the size of the box and cut slots round the edges. Instead of eight I put seven or nine slots and when a cast is wound on the edges are equally covered and the cardboard is less strained out of shape. Finally I place only one cast in each box and carry only three or four. If further changes are desired I change the flies on the cast which takes very little more time. Flies are better carried in a box which is deep and has several divisions. With only two or three flies in each partition little harm will come to them. For large flies I use a fly box of the usual type.

Dyeing Feathers and Hackles

Although nature provides us with a superabundance of fly-tying materials in almost every shade and hue in the spectrum, they are not all easily come by. Those, which are really rare are expensive, but alas some which are not so rare are made to seem so, so that the price can be kept up. However, do not be despondent as you can acquire quite a wide range of such materials by seeking around. The poultry dealer can be approached around the festive season, when particular birds are being prepared for the special tables. I have the advantage of residing in the country and have been fortunate to become known as a keen angler and a tier of artificial flies. I have only to say the word and many types of suitable feathers are forthcoming. However, when I have difficulty in obtaining some specially coloured types mostly for hackles, I prepare for a session at dyeing feathers of many sizes. I seek neck feathers (hackle) and a few wing and tail feathers from a white leghorn hen or cockerel or from some other white breed and when I have gathered the necessary equipment the work of dyeing can begin. **The sketches in Figure 7.6 for show the details.**

Preparing the Hackles

The hackles are prepared in the following manner :
Strip the hackles from the neck-cape and **grade** them into three different sizes meantime. A much finer grading can be done when the dyeing process has been completed. **Tie** them into bundles of not more than ten. Use a strong cotton thread leaving enough thread to take a small weight, such as a nail as indicated. *Prepare a solution of 12 parts water to one of vinegar in a wide flat container and submerge the small bundles in the solution .* The solution will act quicker if the water is slightly heated. Stir vigorously. The feathers will tend to float due to the tiny quantities of air trapped between the

Elements of Angling

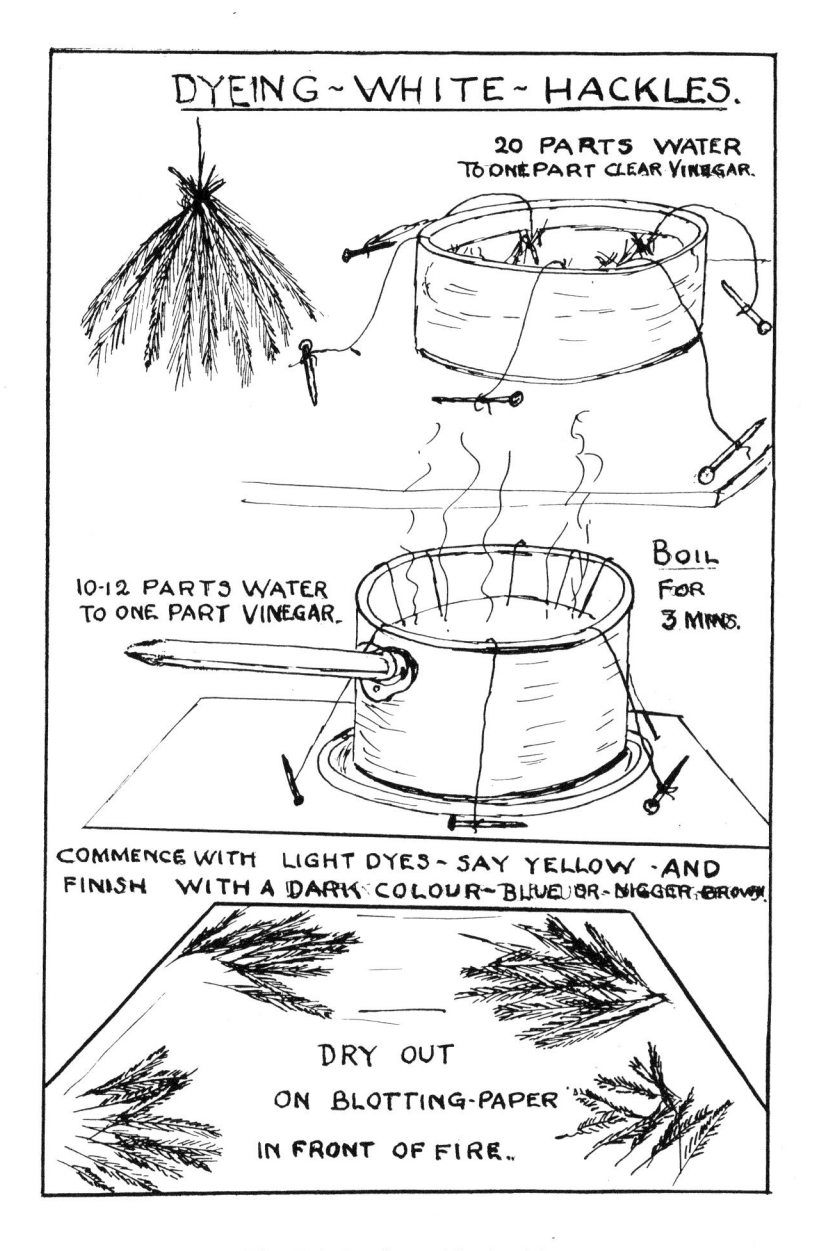

Fig. 7.6 Dyeing white hackles

fibres. Take a fork or spoon and keep prodding them until you are satisfied that all the air is expelled and the natural oil has been washed out. They should be left in the solution for a few minutes and before lifting out, should be wafted to and fro until they are completely soggy. There is not so much oil on the feathers taken from a cockerel as those on the corresponding hen, but very much more on the feathers of any kind of water bird. In the case of the cockerel hackle there should be a greater degree of sparkle on them and the cleaning of them in this way ensures that maximum sparkle is maintained. I believe that the thorough cleaning is as important as the dyeing itself.

The dyeing solution is now prepared. A pan, which I recommend should be an old one and after use, should be well cleaned and put aside for the same use in the future. Have it filled with water and vinegar 12 parts to one approximately. Bring it to the boil. Select the dye. If it is intended to have a long session of dyeing, select the lightest colour first and follow on with the next darker colour to be used. The results obtained have caused me to prefer some types of dyes to others for certain colours. For example for yellows and greens *Fairy* dyes were used, for browns and maroons *Jiffy* dyes were preferred, for shades of blue – *Drummer* dyes proved to be best and for greys, black or reds to give the best sparkle – *Soloid* photographic stain was excellent, but some of these trade names are no longer on the market. However, good results can still be obtained by using any one type of dye for all the colours.

Some of the dyes may give fair results by following the instruction to use cold water, but I have found that the boiling usually makes the colour last longer, while being fished.

Back to the dyeing – take a small pinch of the dye – not more than would cover the nail for the little finger is now added. Do not stir – the boiling will do that for you. Do not allow it to boil too vigorously as it might sputter over. You hope to dye feathers only. Lower the bundles of hackle into the solution gently, one at a time. About three bundles of each size could be done at the same time and after simmering for two or three minutes they should be lifted out again. A few wing and tail feathers, which have already been prepared can now be dyed before the colour is changed. When done, both hackles and feathers can be dried on blotting paper before a radiator – spread out singly. Do not use newspaper as some of the print may blemish the true colours. do not attempt to rinse off the vinegar. I have not found that the vinegar does any damage as has been suggested by some. On the other hand I feel that the colours last longer in the water if the flies are made from feathers which have not been rinsed after dyeing. Please note: I think hackles from a cockerel are superior to hackle taken form the hen of the same breed on two counts: (1) The cock hackles have a better sparkle (2) the cock hackle

Elements of Angling

moves more life-like in the water, whereas the hen hackles being softer, cling more closely to the body of the fly. Try little experiment for yourself – for example take a cast of flies and move the flies about in a basin or bath with ample water and observe closely how each behaves. Much can be learned in this way.

Line Driers

Good lines cost a fair amount of money and it is desired that they last for more than a season or two. Thus you will find on illustration sheet Figure 7.7 and 7.8 give details for two easily made line-driers. Anyone with a fretsaw and the same tools as mentioned in earlier pages should find little difficulty in making them. In the top one all sizes are indicated but these may be altered to suit the materials you have to hand. Nail the two pieces of plywood together for shaping with the fretsaw. Small pilot holes can then be drilled at the five places indicated and the edges of the wood marked for guidance when assembling the parts. Larger holes can be at the centre and where the turning handle is to be. Cut 4 pieces of dowel rod to exactly the same length and square the ends and make a starting hole with a brad awl for screws about 1/2" by 4. Screw parts together except for one screw.

Prepare the handle as shown and drill a hole right through it so that a long thin screw can pass through it loosely, through the plywood into the dowel. The central spindle is put through a hole of suitable size, but is fixed by means of a screw with a washer on the handle side and located on the other side by means of a nail or split-pin in a hole through the spindle. A wire ring is inserted from each side of a hole near the end and squeezed together. This ring helps to hold the article while winding and can also be used to hang up the whole concern while the line is drying. The handle could be fixed by using a double ended screw – the type used to fix the handle to a walking stick.

This idea is given in the hope that the raw angler might be encouraged to design a drier for himself. Therefore look at the example shown at sketch below No. 7.7 and 7.8. How about that for a very simple design?

Anyone who has access to a small turning lathe for metalwork might be able to construct a line-drier entirely made of aluminium or other suitable metal. (Figure 7.9) The illustration is one made to a similar design and size as given in Figure No. 7.7.

Elements of Angling

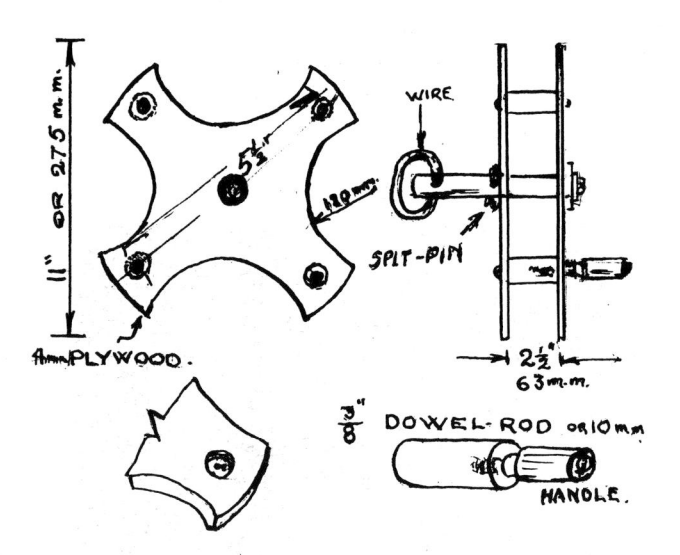

Figure 7.7 Easily made line drier in Wood

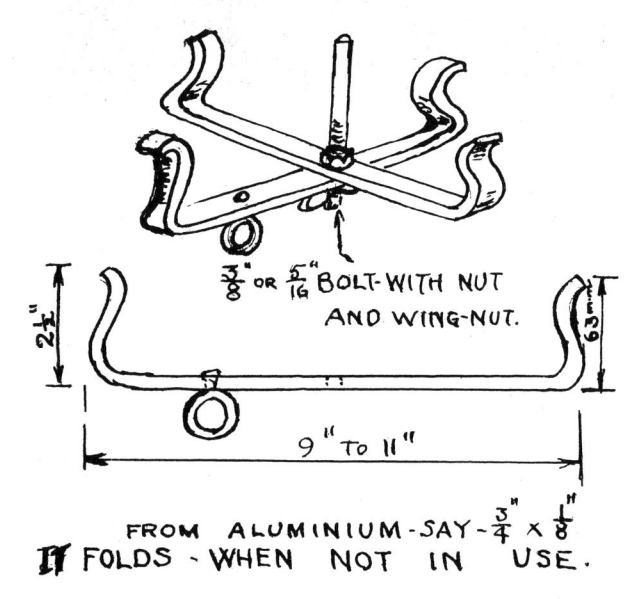

Figure 7.8 Easily made line Drier in Metal

Fig. 7.9 Aluminium Line Drier

8
THE LIFE CYCLE OF THE SALMON

The Spawning

It is a known fact that salmon gather at the river mouths throughout most of the season, waiting for the opportunity, when the heavy waters come, to ascent to the spawning beds in the upper burns and smaller tributaries. We have the early springers followed be a succession of runs with each of the intermittent heavy flows from the usual rains. Most of the fish do not spawn until the late Autumn and some may spawn as late as November. It is really surprising that fish should enter the rivers so many months before spawning and more so when we learn that salmon do not feed in fresh water. There are many theories put forward for this and I have one of my own, which may be of interest. Many salmon to their misfortune, take an artificial minnow in mid stream, a worm on the river bed or rise to an artificial fly near the surface. All these are food stuffs, which they had taken when they were younger and when they were living solely in fresh water. They still attempt to take them, but my idea is, that when once they have tasted salt water with their food at sea they decidedly will not swallow any food unless it is accompanied with salty flavours. Their throats, due to some uncontrollable reactions of the muscles, will not open the gullet. It refuses to swallow. Thus many morsels of food are taken, sucked, and are then rejected. Therefore no food reaches the stomach while they are in fresh water.

The early fish leave the sea with the eggs or milt only slightly formed and these fish are very strong, because their flesh is very healthy and well charged with energy, but as it spends time in the fresh water gradually its healthy fatty oils go to form the eggs or milt as the case may be and all the while the fish does not take any more food. To me this is one of the most striking facts of nature.

From mid-summer on, this goes on while they are waiting in deep pools mostly at the necks or the run outs, where they are exposed to river pollution, disease, and to the carnivorous otter, the mink and not least river netters and the angler also accounts for many of their number.

When all these losses are considered I feel that it is very surprising that nature manages to nurse any survivors at all. The self imposed "hunger strike" for several months while the spawn is being formed must make them weaker and weaker, yet we all know how they will put up a brave fight; strong and lasting that they might survive to do their spawning in the end. Within recent years restocking with salmon fry is being carried out in varying ways. However it is customary to find that the early salmon spawn in the head streams and tributaries, while those that run later usually spawn in the upper reaches of the river itself. The spawning fish look for a gravel bed with stones the size of golf balls or more, which can easily be moved around, which is done by the hen fish to make a redd. There she settles down to lay her eggs. These eggs mostly slip between the stones where they are held against the current and where they are protected from predators, yet where they can be reached by the milt spread from the male (cock) fish, who follows behind to do the fertilising. It happens often that one male fish sprays his milt over more than one redd. When that area of redds have been completed the fish may move further up stream where the hen fish will deposit another quota of ova, varying between 600 and 1000 in another redd with the male attending to his duties in turn. These redds can be located by the disturbed stones which are usually of a lighter colour than the surrounding parts. The eggs are rarely seen, but should you see round jellyballs about 5/16" in diameter sticking together in small clusters do not disturb them. The idea of only depositing a limited quota is nature making sure that there are not too many for the food supplies available at one place and those persons who would do a bit of restocking would do well to take note of this when introducing fry or fish of any size to the water. It would be next to useless to put about 500 fry of say a month old into one spot in a mountain stream. There would not be enough food to go round. Not even sufficient to give them enough energy to swim to another part of the stream to search for food.

All young salmon stay in the fresh water for at least one year, during which they will grow to from 4 to 6 inches. Then they are known as parr. Their development will depend on the health of the stock, the amounts of food available and on the climatic conditions prevailing at that time. In the next year or the next again, they change from the chubby parr with its bar markings to the elegantly lined silvery coloured smolt, in which form they descend to the sea. It has been proved in general, that in the more northern rivers, to reach the smolt stage, takes longer. However, they are very strong and swift for their size. This helps to preserve them from many of their natural enemies. When they reach the salt water it takes a day or so to become accustomed to the change and this is again a time when they run a grave risk of early

Elements of Angling

extermination; the goosander, the cormorant and the heron are among those waiting for them and here too their numbers are depleted once more. What other hazards await them in the deep waters of the ocean, I know not, but rest assured there will be many. However, in two or three years time after they have been nourished by the several foods found at the feeding beds, which are assumed to be located at the south east areas near Greenland, they begin the trail back to the fresh water. Often they return to the river of their birth but not always. It is asumed that a salmon first returns to the fresh water as a grilse. This happens after two to three years at sea and spawns for the first time and if it returns to the sea again and goes back to the river for a second time it is classed as an adult salmon.

Much of the information gained regarding the Life Cycle of the Salmon has been established by the now common method of "Tagging". The expert readings of scale taken from the fish are also a help. When studying scales under the microscope, the expert can tell the age of the fish and any irregularities that may have happened during its lifetime. Should you come across any fish which have been tagged, you should find out where you can report your find. You could be helping in the solving of some of the mysteries involved in the life of the salmon.

9

ANATOMY

Many anglers go through their fishing lives without seeing any need for becoming familiar with the details of fish anatomy and it would appear that ignorance in this aspect of the "piscatorial art" has not interfered with the quantity of fish going into the yawning creel. However, it will be interesting to gain some knowledge on the subject. Illustrations on the plates (9.1, 9.2 and 9.3) give the names of parts of *Salmonidae* (Salmon, seatrout and brown trout – classed as **game fish**) and *Percidae* (the common perch).

Identification of fish can be aided by positions and sizes of parts and certain other characteristics, such as colour permanent or temporary during changes in a fish's development. When I caught the fish of peculiar shape, at first I thought I had taken a rare specimen but on detailed inspection I came to the conclusion that it was a misformed brown trout, which had met with an accident wither at birth or later on in life. It had two kinks in its spine and looked like a hunch–back. It had a large head for its size but had a small rear portion compared to a normal trout. I feel that, this fish having gone through life with this disability, demonstrates the survival capability of the species.

If we become familiar with the anatomy of fish, we are more able to discuss and communicate to others, where disease or fungus has first taken effect or some other circumstances. Only recently I was approached by a friend, who had caught a fine example of a freshly run seatrout. It was $6^1/_2$ lbs. in weight – a real beauty, but just behind the left pectoral fin there was a peculiar mark about the size of a new penny. At first it was thought to be a mark made by a gaff and that the fish had regained its freedom at the landing, but it was later assumed that the mark had been caused by a lamprey attaching itself to the fish to suck its blood. This predator usually frequents the brackish water at the river mouths and while it is attached to a fish it cannot take water through its mouth for "breathing" purposes; instead it breathes through a short row of holes, near its head arranged like a row of port--holes on ship. In some localities it is known as a "Lantern–eel".

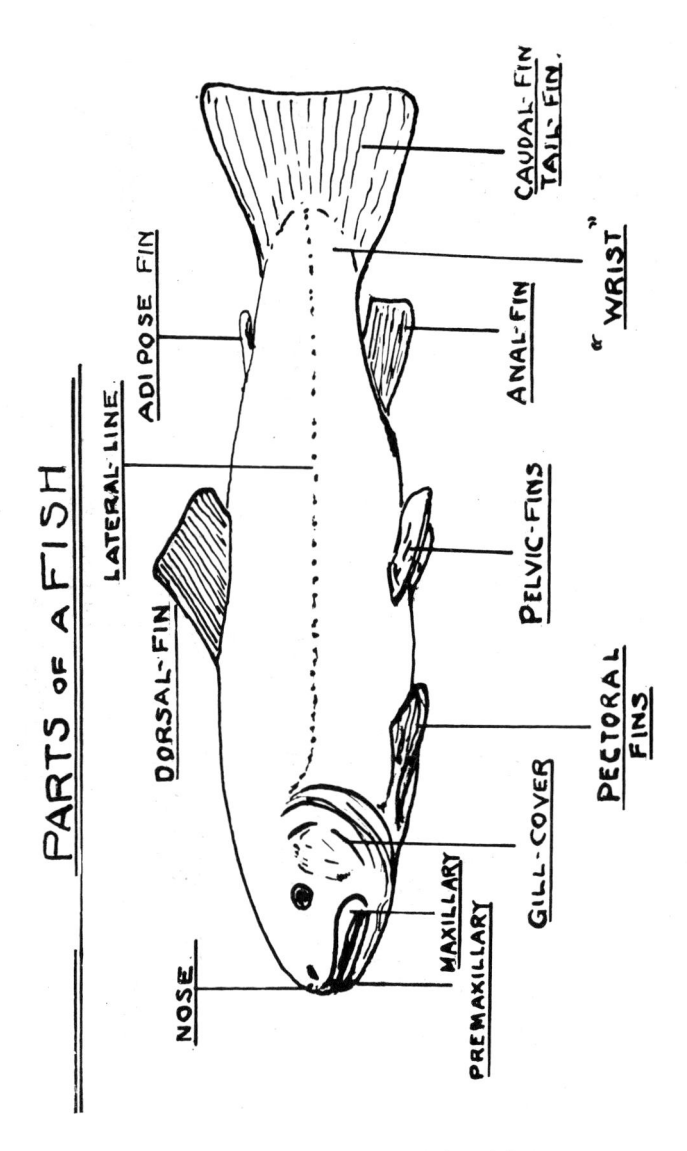

Figure 9.1 Parts of a Fish
Proportions as for most Salmonidae

Elements of Angling

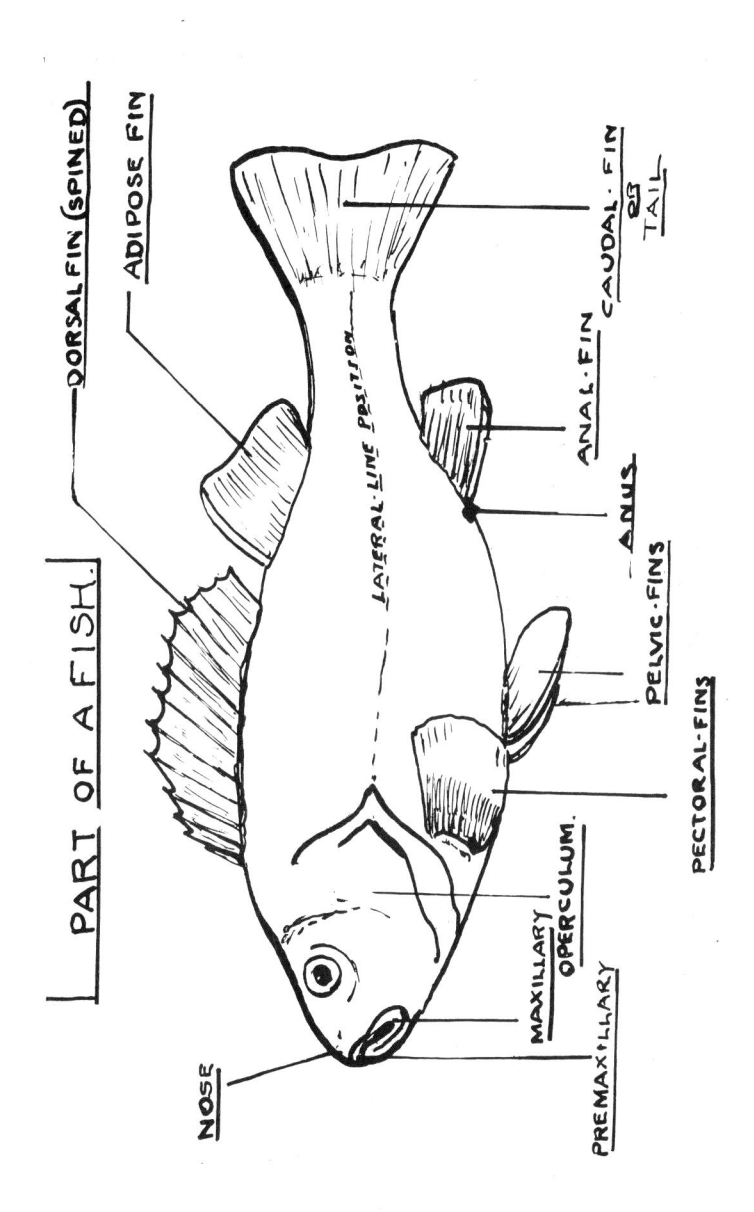

Figure 9.2 Parts of a Fish
Proportions as for Percidae

Elements of Angling

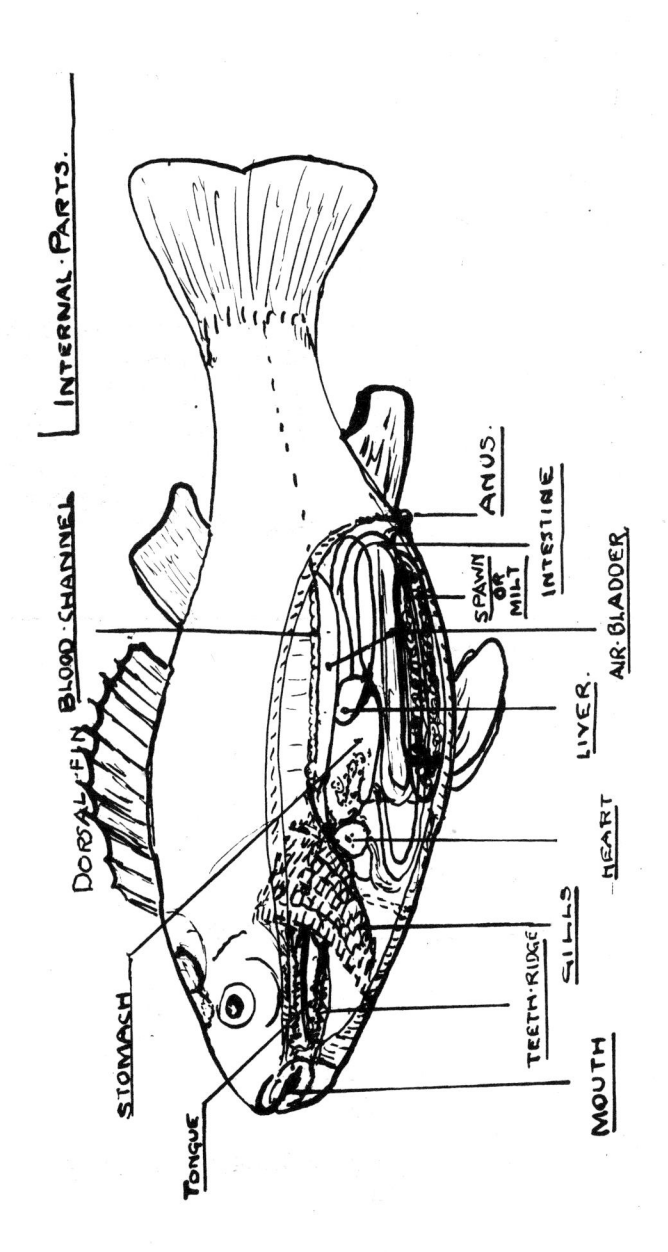

Figure 9.3 Internal Parts

Elements of Angling

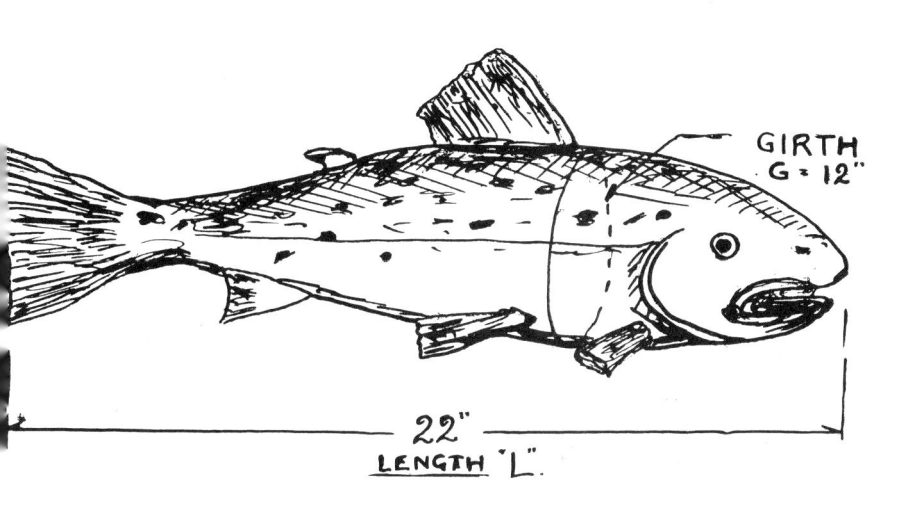

Figure 9.4 Method to Estimate Weight

Formula

$W = (\frac{1}{2}G)^2 \times L$ divided by 200

We have :

$$W = \frac{6^2 \times 22}{200} =$$

$$= \frac{36 \times 22}{200} = 3.96\text{lb.; ie, 4lb. approx.}$$

SPRING SALMON ARE STRONGER

It is common knowledge that in most cases the spring salmon puts up a far superior fight to the fish which comes up later in the season. I was approached on this subject not so very long ago, and on the spur of the moment I muttered something about the fish being stronger and left it at that. Later, I gave more consideration to the question; and now I put forward what I feel are the reasons for this seemingly strange phenomenon.

In all probability, spring fish are descendants of spring fish. Therefore, each generation will arrive early at the estuaries after the long thriving visits to the feeding grounds, which, for the Atlantic salmon, are now considered to be off the South-East coast of Greenland.

Some anglers claim that they can tell the difference in the shape of the earlier type compared to the later arrival. Quite a number are convinced there are two different species. Be that as it may, we are discussing the fighting qualities of the salmon which ascend our rivers, and I think my conjecture remains valid, even given that there could be some differences in the pedigrees. For our purposes, let us assume that all salmon in our streams are one and the same. It would appear that salmon arrive at some of our estuaries so early that they encounter some of the spent fish returning to the feeding beds to be "made up" again, while the fresh fish are waiting with strong, muscular bodies to ascend at the first sign of a spate.

If one of them is actually caught and examined, it will be found, except in very exceptional cases, that the spawn and milt are not far advanced in development and is therefore much smaller in bulk than it will be later. Should the fish, instead of being caught, remain some time in the estuary and is unable to ascend the river, due to lack of water then that same fish's muscular flesh, will be gradually changed to spawn, since we are all of the opinion that salmon do not feed in fresh water. This obscure, almost metamorphic change must take place within the fish itself. To me it is inevitable that this healthy flesh is gradually changed to regenerating organisms: spawn and milt. The longer this goes on, there is less flesh and more spawn, and the more the spawn the greater the load to be carried by the less muscular flesh. The earlier in the season that the fish is hooked then the more it will be able to put up the better fight. No matter, be it the Don or the Dee or the Doon where the salmon come to perpetuate their kind, the fighting spirit will vary according to the state of muscular strength remaining as the process of forming spawn advances.

Elements of Angling
Heat Hazard – Thermal Exhaustion

Season 1984 will long be remembered not only for the longest warm spring and early summer on record, it will also be remembered by anglers in many parts of the country for the disastrous effect which that long hot spell brought to many of our rivers, especially those in the south-west of Scotland.
On the second Sunday of June, two keen anglers came to my door in a panic. They gave me the tragic news that someone or something hadpoisoned one of our local burns, and that many dead and dying fish lay at the edges of several shallow pools. Since a few of them showed by their movements that they still had the desire to live, these two anglers collected several and transferred them to the parent river some 150 yards away. Their quick action was rewarded when they watched most of them recover slowly and win their way to the deeper water. One of these gallant fellows asked me to contract Clyde Purification Board to have the water tested. However I myself ventured to give a solution to this strange problem. The temperature of the water in the shallow burn had risen to such an extent that there was not sufficient oxygen in it to sustain fish life. This is exactly what the representative of the Purification Board stated later. The name given to this exceptional phenomenon is "Thermal Exhaustion". A few days later as the intense heat continued, the main river became affected and on page 124 a photograph shows the extent of the damage caused by such extreme conditions – 4 salmon, 1 sea-trout, 5 rainbow trout and three parr were lifted from a shallow pool while others were able to move slowly out of reach. Others were returned to deeper water but were observed to gasp very actively for water containing sufficient of the life-giving oxygen to survive. For several days afterwards folk were reporting to me to obtain assurance that the water had not been poisoned. It was really cause for panic, but realising the true cause many were relieved for with poisoned water, all river life would have been affected and it would have taken years to recover. Although instances of such misfortune to fish stocks will occur only rarely in this part of the world, where long spells of extra hot weather conditions are exceptional, yet riparian owners would do well to remember the 1984 heat-wave in Scotland and make some provision to protect their fish stocks. What provision can be made? Some will ask. No one can provide protection on such a large scale? Granted – not a good deal can be done, nevertheless. Since it is assumed that the direct rays of the sun are the major factor in this Thermal Exhaustion hazard, if shade can be supplied for small areas of a few pools, some protection can be gained. It is believed that fish in very deep pools are, to some extent, protected by the depth of the water, but during excessive heat the oxygen is much less throughout the water and fish, in order to get their oxygen supply tend to rest in or near streamy water. If that is the case, then

Fig. 9.5 Death from Thermal Exhaustion

owners should concentrate their efforts to provide some protective shade in the shallower pools and holding runs. How can this best be done? It is really a long-term project. Trees and bushes should be planted on the banks close to the water's edge. Some anglers will be shocked to learn that the planting of trees has been recommended. This is suggested with reservations: (1) that they are trimmed in such a way that they do not grow tall, but are actually trained to spread out over the water to give shade; (2) or trees can be grown for a few years and may become quite tall and when they become of such a size that one cannot pass a rod from one hand to the other, round the trunk, while following to continue to play an attached fish, then that tree should be cut down and replaced with a younger one.

Willow growths are easily trained to give good shade yet they seldom reach awkward dimensions. Thorn of any kind should not be used as they will cause tangled lines. Tall grass gives edge shade late and early in the day but no protection when the sun is overhead – during the mid day sun. All these factors should be borne in mind during bank trimming and management.

Restocking

So extensive and demanding has the sport of angling become, that the natural stocks, especially of game fish, have become considerably depleted. So much so that many riparian owners have resorted to restocking. This replenishing of fish stocks is now being practiced on a vast scale and is being done in several well established ways. One of the methods I deplore very much, is what might be called "put and take" system, where fish of mature sizes are distributed, mostly in still water a night or two before a competition is held. The fish have not had time to settle in their new environment, when lures closely resembling their former food stuffs are presented to them and to which they fall prey too easily. In other instances, however, adult fish are being distributed at secretly chosen places. These fish have been purchased from a fish farm. This is perhaps the most popular method, but others with the expert know how have established hatcheries of their own, purchased "eyed-ova" – eggs which have been fertilised, and have successfully reared young fish to be put into their waters at reasonable stages. Still others have sought permission from their respective Fishery Boards to take adult fish at the correct time of season, so that spawn, i.e. ova from the hen fish and milt from the cock fish, can be brought together to be fertilised and then spread on wide meshed trays and placed under running water to hatch them. When about four weeks old and only about two centimetres long and still attached to their egg sacks, which supplies them with nurture at the beginning, they can be distributed in the smallest upper streams feeding the parent rivers or lochs. Some of these hatcheries, which have the added facilities, can rear them until they are of fingerling size or more, before having them dispersed in suitable places in small numbers at a time.

After all the careful work in obtaining adult fish, stripping the spawn fertilising and hatching small healthy fish it is still necessary to exercise care right up to the distribution time. There have been occasions when young fish have been lost by being introduced too suddenly to their new habitat. In the case of tiny fish still attached to their egg sacks, a sudden change of temperature can be disastrous. Game fish in particular reach this stage in their development in the spring of the year when the temperature of the tributaries are usually very low. Even with more mature fish an attempt should be made to minimise the sudden shock. One method is shown in the photo. The lads in the centre of the picture are allowing some of the water to flow into the distribution vessel, slowly, a little at a time, and as seen further back the vessel has been tilted slowly to liberate the fingerlings.

Fig. 9.6 One Method of carefully liberating fingerlings

Final Considerations

Should the reader be an individual taking up angling as a pastime or hobby and goes on to be a fully fledged angler, he or she will fall into one of two categories:

1. Those who are always hoping to come home with a bulging creel and to turn that success into personal fame or financial gain; or

2. those who have joined the sport for its recreational value and incidentally becoming acquainted with the ways of nature and although returning from a day's fishing with an empty creel would swear that he or she had enjoyed and benefitted from a sojourn out in the open.

There are other categories into which an angling person could be fitted. he or she may prefer to "major" in :

(a) Bait fishing
(b) fishing , using spinning lures; or
(c) being a "fly-purist".

Whatever the choice, it is hoped that all will take part in the sport in a sensible and considerate manner which will be a credit to the publishing of this book, which the author feels may be considered to be a small contribution to the recognised ways of angling.

May every reader combine commendable skill with good fortune and have what the fraternity knows as "tight lines", for years to come.

INDEX

A
Artificial Flies, 36
Anatomy of the Fish, 117

B
Bait Tackle, 17
Brown Trout, 9

C
Casting, 24, 26 – 29,
    with the fly, 45
Catches, 80
Conditions for Fishing, 81

D
Dapping, 80
Dry Fly Fishing, 75 – 79

E
Equipment, 4–8
Etiquette on the River Bank, 25

F
Flies, 32 – 45
Fly-tying, 22 – 34
Fly-tying Pliers, 30
Feathers for Flies, 38
Fishing at:
    Dusk, 84
    Night, 85
Fishing Times, 87

H
Hackles, 108
    Dyeing, 108–111

K
Knots, 20

L
Landing, 50, 53
Line Driers, 11, 113
Lures, 63

M
Minnows, 63–66

P
Penalties (legal), 56, 57
Pennel Tackle, 18
Perch, 91, 93
Pike, 91, 93
"Playing", 50

R
Records, 96
Restocking, 125

S
Salmon, 114, 122
Salmon & Fisheries Act, 56, 57
Stewart Tackle, 17
Striking, 46–49
Spinning Rod, 60
Spoons, 67–73

T
Trout Rod, 98–106
Thermal Exhaustion, 123

W
Waders, 89
Wading, 89